Dr. Charlotte de Brabandt
Burkard Schemmel

HYPER-LEADERSHIP

HOW GREAT LEADERS ATTRACT, INSPIRE, AND DEVELOP TALENTS AND ELEVATE THEIR SUCCESS

hyper-leadership.com

Second Edition

Bibliografische Information der Deutschen Nationalbibliothek:
Die Deutsche Nationalbibliothek verzeichnet diese Publikation in der Deutschen
Nationalbibliografie; detaillierte bibliografische Daten sind im Internet über
http://dnb.dnb.de abrufbar.

Second Edition

© 2025 Charlotte de Brabandt and Burkard Schemmel

www.hyper-leadership.com

Publisher: BoD · Books on Demand GmbH, Überseering 33, 22297 Hamburg,

bod@bod.de

Print: Libri Plureos GmbH, Friedensallee 273, 22763 Hamburg

ISBN: 978-3-8192-2838-4

About the Authors

Dr. Charlotte de Brabandt's journey to becoming one of technology and negotiation's most influential voices was forged in the crucible of personal adversity. Faced with a cancer diagnosis at a young age, she transformed this profound challenge into a wellspring of strength that would define her unique approach to leadership. Rather than allowing her diagnosis to limit her aspirations, she emerged as a warrior leader whose personal battle taught her invaluable lessons about resilience, authenticity, and the power of embracing vulnerability in professional settings.

This warrior spirit has infused every aspect of her remarkable career. Just as she approached her cancer treatment with determination and strategic thinking, she brings the same focused resolve to her role as Senior Procurement Manager at Amazon Business, where she masterfully oversees strategic initiatives across EMEA and DACH regions. Her authentic leadership style, shaped by her personal health journey, has enabled her to build deep, meaningful relationships with over 129 key customers and reach an audience exceeding 200,000 professionals, including 22,500 C-level executives.

Her experience with cancer taught her that true strength often lies in transparency and human connection – a philosophy she applied during her tenure at Johnson & Johnson, where she led the company's largest energy negotiation in history. Managing a $1 billion spend and achieving 33% global savings in just 4 months, she demonstrated how the resilience and strategic thinking developed during her personal health battle could translate into extraordinary professional achievements.

During eight years with the Volkswagen Group, including her role as Head of Procurement at Porsche Design Timepieces AG, she channeled the same determination that helped her overcome cancer into building a procurement team from scratch and generating €1 billion in savings. Her personal battle with illness taught her the importance of building strong support systems and fostering team resilience – lessons she's applied throughout her career.

Understanding firsthand the importance of support and inclusivity, Dr. de Brabandt has become a passionate advocate for creating supportive professional environments. She serves on the ISM Thought Leadership Council as a Co-Chair and holds executive positions in various Procurement councils. Her three published books on negotiation draw not only from her professional expertise but also from the profound insights gained during her cancer journey.

Her academic achievements, including a Doctorate in Business Administration and an MSc in Philosophy focusing on technology organizational change, are made more remarkable by the perspective she brings as someone who has faced and overcome significant health challenges. As a TEDx speaker and guest lecturer at Rutgers University, she shares not just her professional insights, but also the transformative lessons learned from her personal battle with cancer – teaching others how to turn adversity into advantage.

Dr. de Brabandt's multilingual capabilities and global citizenship (German, Swiss, and US) allow her to share her message of resilience and authentic leadership across cultural boundaries. Her ongoing commitment to both business excellence and medical research, including recent publications on hemophagocytic lymphohistiocytosis treatment, reflects her dedication to making a meaningful impact in multiple fields.

Through her work with philanthropic organizations like the Swiss Red Cross and Lions Club International, she demonstrates that true warrior leadership extends beyond professional achievement to creating positive change in others' lives. Her story stands as a powerful testament to how personal challenges, particularly her battle with cancer, can forge stronger, more empathetic, and more effective leaders in the modern business world.

Dr. de Brabandt's journey from cancer patient to influential business leader illustrates that our greatest challenges can become our greatest sources of strength. Her warrior spirit, forged in personal battle, continues to inspire and transform the business landscape, proving that authentic leadership isn't just about professional expertise – it's about the courage to embrace our vulnerabilities and use them to create positive change.

Burkard Schemmel is a General Manager specialized in B2B Commerce, Technology, and Ecosystem Plays. Burkard has been working for 20+ years in High Tech and Consulting. Being an entrepreneur at heart, he founded 4 companies serving as CxO, helped mid-size organizations to develop new services, consulted large enterprises in strategy, technology, and operations, and ran large technology teams and B2B commerce operations. His focus is on accelerating growth by building global services, ecosystem plays, and 'as-a-service' business models.

During his career, Burkard served in multiple international roles in leadership, program management, and business operations for Fortune 500 companies. His focus is on growth strategies, business origination, and strategic selling. He founded and led a global practice of 900+ cross functional experts in Medical Technology industry, ran business transformation projects, and built digital commerce teams in commercial and public sector. Most recently, Burkard leads the Northern Europe Sales Organization of Maersk.

Burkard believes that business success is based on ethical values. He is co-founder of a non-profit think tank that leads the transformation of our society into an alterocentric market economy. Working with deep tech companies, he connects unicorns with cooperations to sell, partner, and learn from each other.

Burkard has influenced the career of hundreds of professionals and grew some of the most versatile business leaders. As executive sponsor for leadership programs, Burkard drives organizations towards sustainability, sovereignty, and societal value. As thought leader, author, and speaker Burkard is known for Corporate Strategy, B2B Commerce, and Business Ethics. He has published several books in German and English.

Burkard holds a diploma in Business Information Systems and worked in the USA, Singapore, Japan, and various EU countries. Burkard collects contemporary art, is passionate about nature, and enjoys cooking with family and friends.

Table of Contents

Foreword by Susan Marty
Chief Product Officer, Institute for Supply Management (ISM)

The Dawn of Hyper Leadership

Western societies stand at a pivotal crossroads, where rapid technological advancement converges with unprecedented demographic transformation. This intersection has created both extraordinary opportunities and complex challenges for organizations of all sizes and sectors. The traditional leadership paradigms that served businesses well in the past are proving increasingly inadequate in this new landscape of constant change and diversity.

Over the last decade, I have witnessed this dramatic evolution firsthand in the procurement and supply chain profession. What once revolved around efficiency, control, and hierarchical decision-making has shifted toward agility, influence, and human-centered transformation. This transformation reflects the broader organizational reality that leadership is no longer about position - it's about presence and adaptability in an increasingly complex world.

The emergence of Hyper Leadership represents a fundamental shift in how organizations must approach talent, innovation, and competitive advantage. Unlike conventional leadership models that often prioritize hierarchical structures and homogeneous thinking, Hyper Leadership embraces the full spectrum of human diversity as a catalyst for organizational success. This approach recognizes that in an era of global connectivity and rapid innovation, the inclusion of diverse talents isn't merely a social imperative – it's a business necessity.

The challenges facing modern organizations are multifaceted. Artificial intelligence and automation are reshaping entire industries. Remote work has transformed traditional office dynamics. Demographic shifts are creating the most diverse workforce in history. Global competition has intensified, and customer expectations have evolved dramatically. In this complex environment, organizations that fail to adapt their leadership approaches risk becoming obsolete.

Hyper Leadership addresses these challenges by leveraging diversity as a strategic advantage. It recognizes that innovation springs from the collision of different perspectives, experiences, and ways of thinking. When organizations actively include and empower diverse talents, they gain access to a broader range of solutions, deeper market insights, and enhanced creative capabilities. This inclusive approach to leadership doesn't just promote social equity – it drives business performance.

At ISM, we are deeply invested in cultivating ethical, strategic, and human-centric leadership. I see firsthand the incredible impact that empowered, inclusive leaders have on their teams, their businesses, and their communities. This experience reinforces the theoretical framework presented in this book and validates its practical applications across diverse organizational contexts.

This book serves as both a theoretical framework and a practical guide for organizations navigating this transformation. It examines why traditional leadership models are insufficient for today's challenges and demonstrates how Hyper Leadership can create more resilient, innovative, and successful organizations. Through detailed analysis and real-world examples, we explore how companies can implement Hyper Leadership principles to:

- Harness the power of diverse perspectives for enhanced innovation
- Build more adaptable and resilient organizational structures
- Develop more effective approaches to talent acquisition and retention
- Create inclusive cultures that drive performance and engagement
- Navigate the complexities of global markets and diverse customer bases

The solutions presented in this book are grounded in both theoretical research and practical experience. They offer actionable strategies for organizations at every stage of their diversity and inclusion journey, from those just beginning to recognize the importance of inclusive leadership to those seeking to enhance existing programs.

As we progress through the 21st century, the ability to effectively implement Hyper Leadership principles will increasingly distinguish successful organizations from those that struggle to remain relevant. This book provides the insights, tools, and frameworks needed to make this crucial transition.

The chapters that follow will guide readers through understanding the foundations of Hyper Leadership, implementing effective strategies, overcoming common challenges, and measuring success. Whether you're a CEO leading a global corporation, a manager seeking to build more effective teams, or an HR professional responsible for organizational development, this book offers valuable insights for navigating the future of leadership in an increasingly diverse and dynamic world.

The time for Hyper Leadership has arrived. Organizations that embrace this approach will find themselves better equipped to thrive in an era of unprecedented change and opportunity. Those that don't risk falling behind in an increasingly competitive global marketplace where effective leadership and strategic vision are no longer optional - they're essential for survival and success.

Introduction

Increasing importance of Hyper Leadership in companies

A process is taking place in Germany that poses and will pose major challenges for companies for years, if not decades, to come. But the Federal Republic is not alone in this. Most Western Countries are experiencing the same development. We are talking about demographic change. People's life expectancy is increasing, while the birth rate is falling. This has an impact on all areas of society, from social security and the healthcare system to the education system. Above all, one of the most important basic elements of society, the economic system, is affected. This is because companies are finding it increasingly difficult to find sufficient and suitable staff.

The European Commission is also concerned about Europe's demographic development. Not least, the shrinking population is reducing the continent's share of the global population. But above all, the Commission wants to counteract the threat of declining economic output. It therefore developed a concept with four pillars, which it presented in 2023. These are: the compatibility of work and family life, support for the younger generation in accessing the labor market and housing as well as political measures for the deployment and retention of older generations in the labor market. The fourth pillar has the addition "if necessary". It provides for managed legal migration to mobilize talent (Commission.europa 2023).

On the other hand, there are numerous findings that clearly show a great need beyond these four pillars. There is also an urgent need for much better inclusion of diverse people in companies, in addition to significantly improving the participation of women. After all, demographic change is not the only problem. There is also a serious acceleration in the development of technical achievements and their application, which no company can avoid. As a result, companies are faced with two serious lines of development that threaten to leave them with a qualitatively and quantitatively inadequate workforce if they do not fundamentally change their business models.

Looking at the role of Hyper Leadership in the modern workforce, the structural changes resulting from demographic processes alone mean that companies must respond to the individual disposition of their employees in order to remain successful in the market. They must find, promote and retain talent. Even the recruitment of suitable people will no longer be possible without the inclusion of diverse individuals. This challenge is not merely a matter of HR strategy; it requires a transformation in leadership — specifically, the rise of Hyper Leadership.

Hyper Leadership goes beyond traditional leadership models by embracing agility, inclusivity, and digitalization. It is no longer enough for leaders to be decision-makers; they must become facilitators of empowered, diverse, and self-organizing teams. Hyper Leadership ensures that organizations are fast, flexible, and future-ready, creating environments that attract and retain the best minds regardless of background, gender, or origin.

The general importance of leadership cannot be overestimated. For the customer base, it is important to increasingly and consistently include the natural leadership of people. People of different ages have different approaches and needs, as do people with disabilities. People of different ethnic backgrounds have different ideas, experiences and requirements for goods and services. The same applies to different genders. These and other differences in core areas of personality often lead to neglect and unjustified judgments, which in turn lead to discrimination. Hyper Leadership actively dismantles these biases by fostering an environment where equal treatment is ensured, and every individual disposition is taken seriously and respected.

Looking at Hyper Leadership in the age of Digitalization, at the same time, rapid technological development, currently culminating in artificial intelligence (AI), is bringing about far-reaching changes. Without automation and the use of technological tools, including robots, no business can survive in the long term. In addition, product development must increasingly adapt to differentiated needs within the customer base if customer groups are to be retained and expanded. Hyper Leadership plays a decisive role here, as diverse people make up a large part of the customer base. Leaders in the hyper-digital age must be capable of integrating human and artificial intelligence to achieve optimal results. The future of leadership will not be defined by hierarchy but by how well companies can leverage AI and automation while maintaining human-centric values.

From family businesses to medium-sized and large companies, an entrepreneurial spirit is needed that knows how to realign itself. Where there used to be rigid levels that communicated instructions - if not orders - from the top down, flat hierarchies are now needed. These structures foster collaboration, rapid decision-making, and continuous learning — all hallmarks of Hyper Leadership.

Today's established knowledge society alone requires that companies reorient to factors such as speed and efficiency, as they form the basis for economic assertiveness in competitive market positions. Knowledge can no longer be limited to company management but is an essential factor across the entire organization. A differentiated workforce is required to ensure broad and in-depth knowledge and to translate it into concrete actions. In addition to consistent training and further education, this can only be achieved with the involvement of diverse, self-directed teams.

There has been a shortage of talent in German - and European - companies for years. However, competent employees are necessary to withstand competition, let alone secure a resounding competitive advantage. Management should recognize that it must embrace Hyper Leadership to build a modern corporate structure and culture that remains adaptable to the demands of the times. Leadership is not just a resource; it is a business imperative.

Hyper Leadership also complements sustainability and environmental responsibility. A corporate culture in which mutual recognition prevails also addresses the highly topical issue of acting in an ecologically responsible manner. The most successful way to adapt the value chain to sustainability is for the company to implement effective leadership at all levels. Strategic vision, digital fluency, and sustainability are intertwined, and Hyper Leadership is the glue that binds them together.

Of course, such processes take time, and the balance between economically necessary decisions and the challenges posed by the demand for sustainability must be constantly realigned. However, it is not only ethical responsibility that leads to the avoidance of environmental sins. Recycling and the elimination of plastic as a general social task has now entered the public mindset. Many people are also asking about the production conditions of an item and the type of resources used. It is therefore becoming increasingly important for companies to take these factors into account from the outset in order to meet the requirements of a modern clientele. In addition, there are increasingly differentiated legal regulations that need to be complied with.

The future of Hyper Leadership says it all, companies need diverse people within the company simply because there are diverse people in the customer base. Many companies are internationally networked. This is another reason why they need people with knowledge from different parts of the world. The great advantage of a diverse workforce is also the unbeatable strength of hyper-adaptive teams that can pivot, innovate, and lead markets forward. Studies have consistently shown that diverse teams achieve the best results. They are characterized by innovative strength, inspiration, high levels of knowledge, and ideal mutual complementarity. Their results serve the fulfillment of needs, increase efficiency, and ensure operational growth.

An entrepreneurially sensible corporate structure therefore involves taking good care of employees. This ranges from various company benefits to empowering autonomous teams with decision-making authority. Employees must not only know but also feel that they are welcome and valued. Diverse talents are often still waiting to be discovered, not least because they are still chronically underestimated due to traditional leadership biases.

Hyper Leadership is the key to unlocking this potential. It is time for companies to clear away the obstacles that prevent true innovation and remove the barriers that limit talent. This is the great entrepreneurial, social, and promising task of leadership in a globalized world. As Confucius said, "The man who cleared the mountain was the same man who began to move small stones aside." Hyper Leadership is the necessary force to move those stones and shape the future of business.

Hyper Agility: The Key to Unlocking the Full Potential of Leadership

In today's rapidly evolving business landscape, organizations face the dual challenge of developing effective leadership while maintaining competitive agility. Hyper agility emerges as the critical solution that bridges these seemingly separate challenges, transforming leadership from an organizational function into a powerful competitive advantage.

Hyper agility provides the organizational framework needed to fully leverage diverse talent pools. Through flexible structures and adaptive processes, it creates an environment where diverse perspectives can flourish and contribute meaningfully to organizational success. This approach is particularly crucial during economic uncertainty, where diverse thinking and rapid adaptation become essential survival tools.

Hyper agility integrates with leadership through several key mechanisms. Flexible team structures enable dynamic team composition based on skills and perspectives, allowing organizations to rapidly reconfigure teams to meet changing needs. These structures create abundant cross-cultural collaboration opportunities and promote inclusive project leadership roles, ensuring that leadership talent is deployed optimally across the organization.

Adaptive communication systems represent another critical integration point. These systems incorporate multi-channel communication platforms that accommodate different communication preferences and styles. They establish language-inclusive policies that remove barriers to full participation, while emphasizing cultural sensitivity in messaging to ensure that communications resonate across diverse audiences. Additionally, these systems prioritize accessible information sharing, democratizing access to critical knowledge throughout the organization.

Responsive decision-making processes complete the integration framework. These processes implement inclusive consultation approaches that gather input from multiple perspectives before decisions are finalized. They establish quick feedback loops that allow for rapid course correction when needed. By integrating multiple perspective integration techniques, these processes ensure that decisions benefit from diverse viewpoints. Finally, culturally aware decision frameworks help leaders navigate complex cross-cultural considerations when making important choices.

The integration of hyper agility and leadership manifests in several practical applications. In talent management, hyper agility enables organizations to quickly adjust recruitment strategies to reach diverse talent pools, expanding access to leadership potential. Organizations can create flexible career paths that accommodate different cultural perspectives, ensuring that leadership development isn't constrained by rigid progression models. Adaptive training programs that respect diverse learning styles help develop leadership capabilities across different segments of the workforce. Finally, responsive mentoring systems provide personalized development support that adapts to individual needs and backgrounds.

Project execution benefits significantly from this integrated approach. The framework supports rapid team assembly based on diverse skill sets, ensuring that projects have access to the optimal mix of capabilities. Cultural intelligence in project planning helps anticipate and address cross-cultural challenges before they impact execution. Flexible work arrangements accommodate different needs, allowing team members to contribute effectively regardless of personal circumstances. Quick adaptation to diverse market requirements ensures that projects remain relevant in rapidly changing environments.

The innovation process is similarly enhanced through hyper agility. Cross-cultural ideation sessions bring together diverse perspectives to generate breakthrough ideas. Rapid prototyping with diverse user feedback ensures that innovations address the needs of different user segments. Flexible innovation channels provide multiple pathways for ideas to emerge and develop, preventing innovative thinking from being constrained by rigid processes. Multi-perspective problem-solving approaches leverage diverse viewpoints to develop more comprehensive and effective solutions to complex challenges.

In times of economic uncertainty, this integrated approach delivers substantial benefits. It leverages diverse perspectives for market insights, helping organizations identify opportunities that might otherwise be overlooked. The approach enables quick adaptation to changing conditions, allowing organizations to pivot rapidly when market dynamics shift. It creates resilient organizational structures that can withstand economic pressures without compromising core capabilities. Perhaps most importantly, it maintains competitive advantage through innovation, ensuring that organizations continue to differentiate themselves even in challenging economic environments.

Implementing this integrated approach requires focused leadership development. This includes cultural competency training that equips leaders with the skills to effectively engage across cultural differences. Adaptive leadership skills help leaders adjust their approaches based on situational needs and team composition. Inclusive decision-making techniques ensure that leaders can effectively gather and integrate diverse perspectives. Change management capabilities enable leaders to guide their organizations through the transformation required to fully implement hyper agility.

Structural adaptation is equally important for successful implementation. Flexible organizational design creates the foundation for agile operations, removing structural barriers to rapid adaptation. Adaptive work policies accommodate diverse needs while maintaining organizational effectiveness. Inclusive communication systems ensure that information flows freely throughout the organization, regardless of hierarchical position or cultural background. Responsive feedback mechanisms provide continuous input that drives ongoing improvement and adaptation.

Process innovation completes the implementation framework. Agile methodology adaptation tailors agile approaches to the specific needs and context of the organization. Cultural sensitivity integration ensures that processes respect and accommodate cultural differences. Diverse stakeholder engagement brings multiple perspectives into process design and improvement efforts. Rapid response protocols enable quick action when circumstances change, maintaining momentum despite environmental volatility.

Organizations should track several key metrics to assess the effectiveness of their hyper agility implementation. Leadership metrics in flexible teams help evaluate how well leaders perform in dynamic, diverse environments. Innovation outcomes from diverse groups measure the tangible benefits of bringing together different perspectives. Adaptation speed in diverse settings assesses how quickly the organization can respond to changing circumstances. Inclusive decision-making effectiveness evaluates the quality and impact of decisions made through inclusive processes.

The integration of hyper agility and leadership development will become increasingly critical as global markets continue to evolve, creating new challenges and opportunities that require adaptive responses. This integration will grow in importance as workforce demographics shift further, changing the composition and expectations of both leadership teams and the broader workforce. The approach will remain essential as economic conditions remain uncertain, requiring organizations to maintain flexibility and responsiveness. Finally, the integration will become more sophisticated as technology continues to advance, creating new possibilities for agile operations and inclusive leadership.

Hyper agility serves as the essential bridge between diversity management and organizational effectiveness. By creating flexible, responsive structures that can accommodate and leverage diverse perspectives, organizations can transform demographic diversity into a powerful competitive advantage. This approach is particularly crucial in today's uncertain economic environment, where the ability to quickly adapt while maintaining inclusive practices can determine organizational success.

Structure of the Book

This book begins by describing the current situation in which companies find themselves. It is characterized by a globalized world in which the demands on all types of companies are undergoing fundamental change. In Germany, the SME sector is strongly represented, and it is precisely these small and medium-sized enterprises that must adapt if they are to withstand a process that demands ever faster and more effective procedures and results.

Chapter I therefore discusses the expectations and requirements of companies in our time. Fundamental factors that companies will need to adapt to include demographic change, the now established knowledge society and advancing technology. As a result, companies now have to look at their employees differently. They need to communicate their corporate purpose and values well. They must also take into account the fact that employees want to experience their work as meaningful. Furthermore, an innovative company needs new definitions of the necessary qualifications. All of these points can only be fulfilled if the collaboration of diverse people in a company becomes a matter of course.

Chapter II is dedicated to the question of what an innovative form of organization can look like. This concerns a new attitude towards both customers and employees. The factors described in Chapter II must be implemented in the new form. Leadership plays a decisive role here.

Chapter III shows the extent to which diverse talents are indispensable in modern and successful companies. In particular, Leadership in teams within flat hierarchies is becoming the core of a future-oriented structure.

Chapter IV is dedicated to the question of how HR management can realize the acquisition of diverse talent. This concerns not only organizational factors and the application of new methods, but also considerations regarding a company's internal openness towards Leadership.

Chapter V discusses how a company can build a culture that sees Leadership as a matter of course. This requires managers who set a good example. Appreciation of diverse employees should be a common thread running through all levels of the company. However, external support is also an important pillar.

Chapter VI looks at how individual diverse talents can be discovered and promoted. It also shows that companies should examine and adapt their HR planning and measure the progress of Leadership. Intercultural competence must be promoted within the company and a working atmosphere of mutual acceptance must be created. Externally, it should be communicated that the company values and implements Leadership.

Chapter VII looks at how a company can implement leadership in practice. It discusses how non-diverse employees can be included in the process, both through training and teamwork. Possible conflict situations are highlighted. It also provides information on the importance of target agreements, evaluations and appreciation.

Chapter VIII provides a summary and a conclusion. Leadership is a process, an economic necessity, and brings with it clear competitive advantages.

Chapter IX provides information on the legal basis, based on the issue of equality.

Literature
Commission.europa 2023, Demography toolkit, accessed 06.04.2024

Hyper Leadership Vision

1. Survive: Cash is King

In times of uncertainty, survival is the first priority. Without financial stability, even the most visionary companies falter. Leaders must embrace a disciplined approach to cost control, liquidity management, and operational efficiency. This phase is about resilience — ensuring that businesses have the cash reserves and cost structures needed to weather economic storms. Hyper leaders understand that cash is not just a financial metric but a lifeline that fuels future ambitions.

1.1 Case Study IT Services Procurement

For organizations managing a vast portfolio of IT vendors — often exceeding 3,000 suppliers — cost optimization is a critical necessity. One of the most effective strategies is vendor consolidation through synergies and strategic vendor selection. This approach involves a meticulous review of the vendor landscape to identify overlapping services, evaluate performance, and eliminate redundancies. By conducting multiple bidding rounds, organizations can methodically narrow down their vendor base to a select group of strategic partners who offer the best value, innovation, and long-term collaboration potential. The key to success lies in rate card negotiations, leveraging increased contract volume with fewer vendors to secure more competitive pricing and enhanced service levels. However, this cost-cutting initiative is not just about financial metrics—it requires a comprehensive stakeholder management approach. Internal teams must be educated on the benefits of consolidation to overcome resistance to change. Hyper Leaders take a top-down approach, ensuring leadership alignment while fostering trust among procurement teams, IT decision-makers, and operational stakeholders. Moreover, effective communication with strategic vendors is essential to set clear expectations, establish mutually beneficial terms, and create an environment that encourages long-term innovation and efficiency. This transformation not only leads to direct cost savings but also enhances operational agility, reduces contract management complexity, and allows companies to reinvest savings into core digital initiatives, strengthening their market position in an increasingly competitive landscape.

1.2 Use Case II: Cost Cutting

In times of economic pressure, large corporations must focus on cost efficiency to ensure long-term sustainability. Traditional cost-cutting measures, when executed strategically, can unlock significant savings while maintaining operational effectiveness. Three key levers—process optimization, technology-driven automation, and standardization—form the foundation for a sustainable approach to headcount reduction. Additionally, establishing a nearshore shared services center offers a structured way to consolidate expertise and drive further efficiencies. However, executing these changes across multiple European countries presents unique challenges that require careful navigation.

Process Optimization, Technology Automation, and Standardization

The first step in cost-cutting is streamlining internal processes to eliminate redundancies and inefficiencies. By identifying repetitive, manual tasks that can be re-engineered or eliminated, organizations can reduce reliance on human labor while enhancing operational agility.

Technology plays a pivotal role in automating these processes. AI-powered tools, robotic process automation (RPA), and advanced analytics help minimize manual intervention in routine operations, improving accuracy and reducing costs. Standardization across functions and business units further simplifies workflows, eliminating the complexity of localized, customized processes that drive up operational expenses.

Nearshore Shared Services: Bundling Competencies for Efficiency

A strategically placed nearshore shared services center (SSC) can centralize operations, reduce costs, and enhance efficiency. By consolidating support functions—such as finance, HR, IT support, and customer service—into a single center, corporations gain economies of scale, better resource utilization, and streamlined management.

However, executing a nearshore SSC strategy across multiple European countries involves several complexities:

Worker's Council Approval Across Countries. In Europe, any workforce restructuring requires careful coordination with worker's councils, which vary by country in terms of influence and legal requirements. A tailored strategy is essential to engage these councils early, presenting a clear business case that balances efficiency gains with workforce impact. Transparent communication, employee transition support, and negotiated agreements can help facilitate smoother approvals.

Language-Based Task Segmentation. Language barriers must be addressed when consolidating operations across countries. One effective approach is isolating English-speaking tasks from non-English-speaking tasks, allowing cross-border resource pooling for standardized processes while maintaining country-specific support where needed. This segmentation ensures that SSCs can operate efficiently without disrupting customer interactions or compliance-related functions.

Knowledge Retention and Transfer. Transitioning processes to a nearshore SSC risks losing institutional knowledge. A phased transition plan, with structured knowledge transfer programs, detailed documentation, and job-shadowing initiatives, is critical to ensuring continuity. Establishing centers of excellence within the SSC helps retain expertise and fosters continuous improvement.

Data Protection Compliance in AI-Driven Automation. Implementing AI-based automation solutions requires strict adherence to GDPR and other European data protection laws. Organizations must ensure that AI-driven processes comply with data minimization principles, secure personal information, and maintain transparency in AI decision-making. Conducting thorough data impact assessments and engaging legal teams early in the planning phase is crucial for regulatory compliance.

Traditional cost-cutting measures, when executed strategically, can significantly improve corporate financial health. Process optimization, automation, and standardization reduce reliance on manual labor, while nearshore shared services centers centralize operations for greater efficiency. However, a well-planned approach is required to navigate European-specific challenges such as worker's council approvals, language segmentation, knowledge retention, and data protection compliance. By addressing these factors proactively, corporations can achieve sustainable cost savings without compromising operational integrity.

2. Strive: The Power of Talent

Survival alone is not enough – businesses must strive for growth, and this starts with people. The right talent is the driving force behind innovation, execution, and long-term success. In a rapidly changing world, leaders who attract, develop, and empower top talent create organizations that are agile, adaptive, and future-ready. Hyper leadership recognizes that business challenges are ultimately solved by people, not processes, making talent the most valuable asset in any growth strategy.

2.1 Use Case I: PIE Concept

Unlocking Leadership Potential

In today's dynamic professional landscape, success is not simply a matter of technical expertise or working hard. While strong performance is essential, it is not enough to guarantee career progression. Many talented professionals find themselves overlooked despite their hard work, leaving them frustrated as they watch others—sometimes less experienced—climb the corporate ladder. The difference often lies in how individuals position themselves within their organizations. Leaders who advance in their careers understand that success is a combination of three key elements: Performance, Image, and Exposure — the PIE concept.

The PIE concept highlights a fundamental truth: leadership success is built not only on delivering results but also on how individuals are perceived and how visible they are within their professional networks. It provides a structured approach for professionals who aspire to leadership roles, ensuring that their work is recognized, their reputation is carefully managed, and they are given opportunities to influence and contribute at higher levels.

At its core, performance remains the foundation of career success. Strong performance is the baseline requirement — without it, no amount of visibility or branding can create sustainable progress. Organizations thrive when employees demonstrate excellence in execution, consistently achieving goals, solving problems, and driving innovation. The most successful professionals go beyond merely fulfilling their job descriptions; they actively seek ways to improve efficiency, contribute to strategic initiatives, and add value beyond their immediate responsibilities. High performers take ownership of their work, show initiative, and display a problem-solving mindset that sets them apart. However, many professionals make the mistake of assuming that their results alone will speak for them. The reality is that in most organizations, hard work is necessary but not sufficient to secure leadership opportunities.

Beyond delivering results, professionals must also shape their image — the way they are perceived by colleagues, leaders, and stakeholders. Career advancement often depends not just on what someone does but on how others perceive their ability to lead. Image is a reflection of personal brand, professional presence, and leadership qualities. It is about how confidently individuals present themselves, how they communicate, and how they are remembered in key discussions. Those with strong leadership presence tend to inspire trust and command respect, making them natural choices for leadership roles. Developing a compelling image requires professionals to align their behaviors with leadership expectations—demonstrating strategic thinking, showing composure under pressure, and cultivating a reputation for reliability and influence. Those who successfully manage their image position themselves as leaders even before they are formally given leadership titles.

Yet, even those with exceptional performance and a strong image can remain stagnant in their careers if they lack exposure—the visibility necessary for key decision-makers to recognize their contributions. Exposure ensures that the right people within an organization are aware of an individual's skills, achievements, and leadership potential. It is not about self-promotion in the traditional sense, but rather about being actively engaged in high-profile projects, seeking out leadership opportunities, and making contributions that are visible to senior executives. Many professionals fall into the trap of working hard behind the scenes, assuming their efforts will be noticed. However, in reality, organizations are fast-paced environments where recognition often goes to those who make their presence known. Successful leaders seek out mentors and sponsors who advocate for them, engage in strategic networking, and participate in discussions where important decisions are made. Exposure is what ultimately opens doors to leadership opportunities, ensuring that when promotions and key assignments arise, an individual's name is at the forefront of decision-makers' minds.

The PIE concept is not just about individual career advancement—it is also a valuable framework for organizations looking to cultivate leadership pipelines and retain top talent. Companies that integrate the PIE concept into their leadership development programs create an environment where performance is rewarded, professional presence is nurtured, and opportunities are equitably distributed. A strong leadership bench is built not just by identifying top performers, but by ensuring that high-potential employees have the visibility and positioning needed to step into leadership roles when the time comes.

Implementing the PIE concept requires a deliberate and structured approach. Professionals who wish to accelerate their careers must first ensure that they consistently deliver results, establishing a reputation for excellence and reliability. They must then actively shape their professional image, ensuring they are seen as leaders who inspire confidence and trust. Finally, they must seek out opportunities for exposure, making their contributions known and positioning themselves for career growth. For organizations, fostering an environment where performance, image, and exposure are actively developed ensures that leadership selection is not based on subjective visibility alone but on a structured approach that identifies and promotes those with the greatest potential to lead.

By balancing performance, image, and exposure, professionals can take control of their career trajectories, while organizations can ensure they are developing and retaining the best leaders for the future. The PIE concept is a powerful tool for both individuals and businesses alike—one that transforms how leadership potential is recognized, nurtured, and ultimately realized.

2.2 Use Case II: Bar Raising

Talent is the driving force behind business growth, and few companies have institutionalized talent evaluation as rigorously as Amazon. One of the key mechanisms Amazon employs in hiring and promotion decisions is the "Bar-Raiser" program. This concept ensures that every new hire and internal promotion contributes to continually elevating the organization's talent pool. By applying a high and consistent standard, Amazon has been able to maintain a culture of excellence and sustained innovation.

What Is the Bar-Raiser Concept?

The Bar-Raiser program is a structured approach to hiring and promotion in which specially trained employees, known as "Bar Raisers," play a decisive role in evaluating candidates. These individuals are independent of the hiring team and are responsible for ensuring that new hires meet or exceed the company's existing talent level. This approach ensures that talent standards do not erode over time, even as the company scales.

Key Principles of the Bar-Raiser Program

Raising the Talent Bar. Every new hire must be better than at least 50% of existing employees in the same role. This principle ensures continuous talent improvement and prevents complacency in hiring decisions.

Independent Decision-Making. Bar Raisers do not report to the hiring manager and have veto power in hiring decisions. This independence reduces biases and helps maintain a consistent standard across the company.

Focus on Leadership Principles. Amazon's hiring process is deeply rooted in its Leadership Principles. Bar Raisers evaluate candidates against these principles, ensuring alignment with Amazon's culture and long-term goals.

Data-Driven Decision Making. Interviews are structured, with each interviewer focusing on specific competencies and providing detailed feedback. The hiring decision is based on data and behavioral evidence rather than subjective impressions.

How the Bar-Raiser Concept Strengthens Organizations

Building a High-Performing Workforce. By consistently raising the bar, companies prevent talent dilution and cultivate a culture of excellence. Employees are constantly challenged and inspired by their peers, driving performance and innovation.

Enhancing Hiring Objectivity. Independent evaluators remove personal biases from hiring decisions, leading to a more diverse and competent workforce. This objectivity ensures that hires are made based on capability rather than personal preferences or immediate hiring needs.

Long-Term Talent Investment. The Bar-Raiser program prioritizes long-term talent quality over short-term hiring speed. While this may slow down hiring, it leads to stronger teams that deliver sustainable business impact.

Consistent Company Culture. Evaluating candidates based on core company principles ensures cultural consistency, even as organizations grow. Employees who align with key values are more engaged and contribute to long-term success.

Implementing the Bar-Raiser Concept Beyond Amazon

While Amazon has perfected this approach, other organizations can adopt similar principles to strengthen their hiring and promotion processes. Companies should consider:

- Training independent hiring evaluators to uphold talent standards.
- Defining clear leadership principles and integrating them into hiring decisions.
- Using structured, data-driven interview techniques to ensure objective evaluations.
- Prioritizing long-term team quality over immediate hiring needs.

By embedding the Bar-Raiser mindset, organizations can build a workforce that not only meets current needs but also positions them for sustained growth and innovation. Talent is the foundation of business success, and companies that strive for excellence in hiring will ultimately lead in their industries.

3. Succeed: Innovate, Lead and Sell

Sustainable success comes from more than just financial prudence and a strong workforce—it requires bold leadership, relentless innovation, and a sharp focus on sales. Market leadership is won by those who not only anticipate change but actively drive it. Hyper leaders understand that selling is not just a function but a mindset — creating value, building relationships, and positioning their organizations ahead of the curve.

Success in this phase is about seizing new opportunities, scaling intelligently, and shaping the future rather than reacting to it.

3.1 Use Case I: ALICE Concept

Leading with Heart, Vision, and Purpose

In an era where leadership is constantly evolving, the ability to inspire, build trust, and drive meaningful impact has never been more crucial. The traditional, top-down leadership style—focused solely on command, control, and efficiency—is no longer sufficient in today's fast-paced and purpose-driven world. Modern leaders must navigate uncertainty, cultivate deep connections, and drive innovation through authenticity and emotional intelligence.

At the core of this new leadership paradigm lies the ALICE Leadership Model, a framework designed to guide leaders toward sustainable success through five essential principles: Act with Authenticity, Lead with Love, Inspire Others, Create Community, and Engage Purposefully. ALICE is not just a model for leadership—it is a philosophy that fosters trust, strengthens teams, and transforms organizations from within.

Act with Authenticity: The Foundation of True Leadership

Authenticity is the cornerstone of great leadership. Leaders who act with authenticity do not hide behind corporate personas or scripted speeches; instead, they lead with integrity, honesty, and self-awareness. They align their actions with their values, ensuring that every decision they make is guided by a sense of purpose rather than a desire to conform or appease.

Authentic leaders embrace vulnerability, recognizing that admitting mistakes or uncertainties does not signal weakness but rather fosters trust within their teams. Employees and stakeholders respond to leaders who are real—who communicate openly, acknowledge their imperfections, and remain true to their beliefs even under pressure. In an age where transparency is demanded more than ever, authenticity is what differentiates transactional managers from transformational leaders.

Beyond personal integrity, authenticity also means fostering a culture of openness within an organization. When leaders encourage honest dialogue, employees feel empowered to share their ideas, voice concerns, and take ownership of their contributions. This, in turn, drives engagement, creativity, and long-term loyalty.

Lead with Love: Human-Centered Leadership in Action

While traditional leadership models often emphasize discipline and performance metrics, ALICE introduces a radically different yet essential component: love. Leading with love does not imply sentimentality or softness; rather, it signifies a commitment to empathy, compassion, and care.

Leaders who lead with love understand that people are the heart of any successful organization. They recognize the importance of fostering psychological safety, where employees feel valued, respected, and supported. They prioritize well-being, knowing that when people feel cared for, they are more motivated, engaged, and productive.

Leading with love also means making tough decisions with compassion. Whether addressing conflicts, restructuring teams, or setting ambitious goals, leaders who embody this principle ensure that their decisions are guided by fairness, respect, and a long-term vision that benefits both individuals and the organization as a whole.

Inspire Others: The Power of Vision and Influence

Inspiration is what transforms good leaders into extraordinary ones. While authority may command compliance, inspiration sparks action, innovation, and unwavering commitment. Leaders who inspire do not merely direct; they energize, motivate, and instill a sense of purpose in those they lead.

True inspiration comes from having a clear and compelling vision. Great leaders paint a vivid picture of the future—one that excites, challenges, and unites people toward a common goal. They articulate this vision not just in words but through their actions, demonstrating a deep belief in what is possible.

Beyond vision, inspirational leaders empower those around them. They recognize potential in others and nurture it through mentorship, encouragement, and opportunities for growth. Rather than hoarding power, they create environments where individuals feel confident in their ability to contribute and innovate.

Organizations thrive when leaders cultivate inspiration at every level. When people feel deeply connected to a mission, they go beyond executing tasks; they become owners of the vision, working passionately to bring it to life.

Create Community: Building Strong, Connected Teams

In today's globalized and digitally connected world, successful leadership is not about individual achievement—it is about creating a sense of belonging and shared purpose. The ALICE model places strong emphasis on community-building, recognizing that leaders must foster environments where collaboration, trust, and mutual support are the norm.

Community-driven leadership means breaking down silos and encouraging cross-functional collaboration. It means building teams where individuals support one another rather than compete, where success is measured not by individual accolades but by collective progress.

The most effective leaders cultivate cultures where innovation and excellence thrive. They recognize that breakthrough ideas come from collaborative problem-solving, and they actively seek out insights that might otherwise go undiscovered. They create platforms for open discussion, ensuring that every team member feels empowered, engaged, and valued for their contributions.

Strong communities also extend beyond internal teams. Leaders who embrace the ALICE model forge deep relationships with customers, partners, and stakeholders, positioning their organizations as trusted, people-first brands. They understand that long-term success is not just about delivering value—it is about creating lasting connections.

Engage Purposefully: Leading with Meaning and Intent

The final principle of ALICE—engaging purposefully—is what ties the entire model together. Leadership is not just about achieving business objectives; it is about making a meaningful impact. Purpose-driven leaders do not operate reactively or chase short-term gains; they lead with intent, ensuring that their actions align with a deeper mission.

Engaging purposefully means making decisions that are not just profitable but also ethical and sustainable. It means considering the long-term implications of leadership choices, prioritizing both people and the planet alongside financial growth.

Leaders who engage with purpose understand that success is not measured by numbers alone. It is measured by the positive change they create—the lives they impact, the innovations they drive, and the legacy they leave behind.

By embracing purposeful leadership, organizations become more than just businesses; they become movements that inspire customers, employees, and society as a whole.

The ALICE Model as a Blueprint for Sustainable Success

In a world where leadership is often reduced to performance metrics and hierarchical authority, the ALICE model redefines what it means to lead with impact. It recognizes that the most successful and admired leaders are those who act with authenticity, lead with love, inspire others, create strong communities, and engage with deep purpose.

By embedding these principles into leadership development strategies, organizations cultivate leaders who are not just effective but extraordinary — leaders who build cultures of trust, drive transformational change, and create environments where people and ideas flourish.

The ALICE leadership model is not just a theory—it is a call to action for the next generation of leaders. Those who embrace it will not only succeed in their own careers but will leave an indelible mark on their organizations, industries, and the world.

3.2 Use Case II: Business Model Innovation

Innovation is not just about creating new products; it is about redefining how businesses generate value. Business model innovation transforms industries by changing the way companies operate, engage customers, and monetize their offerings. Two of the most impactful examples of business model innovation in recent history are Apple and Tesla. These companies have not only disrupted their respective industries but also established new standards for customer experience and revenue generation.

Apple: The iPhone and the Power of an Ecosystem

Before Apple entered the mobile phone market, manufacturers such as Nokia, Motorola, and BlackBerry dominated the industry. Their business models focused primarily on hardware sales, with incremental improvements in design, battery life, and features. Revenue streams were largely limited to one-time purchases of devices, with minimal integration between products.

Apple revolutionized the industry with the iPhone by shifting from a standalone product model to a comprehensive ecosystem-driven approach. The key innovations included:

Hardware and Software Integration: Unlike competitors, Apple tightly integrated its proprietary iOS with hardware, ensuring a seamless user experience.

App Store and Developer Ecosystem: By launching the App Store, Apple enabled third-party developers to create applications, driving user engagement and opening new revenue streams via app purchases and in-app transactions.

Subscription Services: Apple expanded beyond hardware sales by introducing recurring revenue models such as iCloud storage, Apple Music, Apple Arcade, and AppleCare+.

Interconnected Devices: Apple's ecosystem extends beyond the iPhone, with seamless integration between MacBooks, iPads, Apple Watch, and HomePods, creating high customer retention rates.

Through these innovations, Apple shifted from selling individual products to an ecosystem-driven model that maximizes lifetime customer value.

Tesla has transformed the automotive industry not just by producing electric vehicles but by redefining the way car features are sold and delivered. Traditional automakers historically relied on a linear sales model, where customers paid for specific hardware features upfront. Once a car was sold, there was limited opportunity for the manufacturer to generate additional revenue.

Tesla disrupted this model by integrating software deeply into its vehicles and leveraging over-the-air (OTA) updates to introduce new capabilities. Key elements of Tesla's business model innovation include:

Built-in but Locked Features: Tesla's vehicles come pre-equipped with various features, but customers can unlock them on a subscription or pay-per-use basis. For example, seat heaters or advanced driver-assistance functions can be activated for a monthly fee.

Over-the-Air (OTA) Software Updates: Tesla continuously enhances its vehicles through software updates, adding new features, improving performance, and even adjusting battery efficiency.

Autonomous Driving as a Service: Tesla offers Full Self-Driving (FSD) as an optional upgrade, available for a one-time payment or a monthly subscription, creating an ongoing revenue stream beyond the initial car sale.

Energy and Charging Ecosystem: Tesla monetizes its ecosystem through Supercharger networks, solar energy solutions, and energy storage, further expanding its revenue opportunities beyond vehicle sales.

By shifting revenue generation from one-time purchases to continuous monetization, Tesla has built a scalable and flexible business model that maximizes long-term profitability.

Both Apple and Tesla illustrate how business model innovation goes beyond product differentiation. Apple's ecosystem approach has redefined customer loyalty and revenue generation through services, while Tesla's software-driven model turns vehicles into continuously improving assets with flexible monetization options. Companies that embrace business model innovation can create sustainable competitive advantages, enhance customer engagement, and open up new revenue streams that traditional approaches fail to capture.

1. Status quo: expectations and requirements

Economic processes in our knowledge society are increasingly subject to automation, creating a complex web of challenges and opportunities that demand new approaches to leadership and organizational agility. This transformation extends far beyond simple technological adoption, requiring fundamental shifts in how organizations operate, lead, and adapt to change.

Technological Adaptation and Automation

The acceleration of automation in the knowledge economy has created several parallel demands. Organizations must focus on integration of AI and machine learning into core business processes, while simultaneously pursuing rapid digital transformation across all organizational levels. Enhanced cybersecurity and data protection requirements have become non-negotiable priorities, and continuous technological upskilling of the workforce is essential for maintaining competitive advantage in rapidly evolving markets

Organizational Model Evolution

Companies must embrace new operational models to remain competitive in today's dynamic environment. Strategic outsourcing of non-core functions allows organizations to focus on their key differentiators while leveraging specialized expertise. Dynamic partnering arrangements across global networks create flexible, responsive value chains that can adapt to changing market conditions. Ecosystem-based collaboration models foster innovation through diverse perspectives and complementary capabilities. Virtual and hybrid work arrangements expand talent pools and enhance employee satisfaction, while cross-functional team structures break down silos and accelerate decision-making processes

Expanded Professional Qualifications

The modern workforce requires an expanded set of qualifications to thrive in complex organizational environments. Technical expertise must be combined with well-developed soft skills to ensure effective collaboration and communication. Cross-cultural communication abilities are increasingly valuable in globalized business contexts. Adaptive learning capabilities enable professionals to continuously evolve their skills in response to changing requirements. Digital literacy across multiple platforms is now a fundamental expectation rather than a specialized skill. Change management competencies allow professionals to navigate and lead transformation initiatives effectively

Hyper Leadership Requirements

In this context, hyper leadership emerges as a critical framework for organizational success. Leaders must develop the ability to lead diverse, distributed teams across geographic, cultural, and technological boundaries. Rapid decision-making in uncertain conditions requires both analytical rigor and intuitive judgment. Cultural intelligence and inclusive practices enable leaders to harness the full potential of diverse teams. Balancing automation and human elements ensures technology serves strategic objectives without undermining human creativity and connection. Integration of diverse perspectives and experiences drives innovation and enhances problem-solving capabilities

Hyper Agility Demands

Organizations must develop enhanced agility capabilities to respond effectively to market volatility. Quick adaptation to market changes requires sensing mechanisms that identify emerging trends and opportunities. Flexible resource allocation enables organizations to rapidly shift focus and investment in response to changing priorities. Rapid skill development and deployment ensures teams have the capabilities needed to address new challenges. Dynamic team formation and dissolution allows organizations to configure optimal groups for specific initiatives. Responsive organizational structures provide the foundation for agile operations across the enterprise.

Modern employees increasingly prioritize factors beyond traditional compensation and benefits. They seek clear articulation of company values that align with their personal beliefs and priorities. Commitment to leadership excellence and innovation demonstrates an organization's forward-thinking approach. Sustainable business practices reflect responsible stewardship of environmental and social resources. Work-life integration opportunities acknowledge the holistic nature of employee wellbeing. Professional development pathways signal investment in long-term employee growth. Meaningful work and purpose connect daily activities to larger organizational and societal impact

Working Conditions Evolution

The definition of good working conditions has expanded significantly in recent years. Flexible work arrangements accommodate diverse employee needs and preferences. Mental health support recognizes the importance of psychological wellbeing for sustainable performance. Inclusive workplace practices ensure all employees can contribute fully and authentically. Career development opportunities maintain engagement and build organizational capability. Technology-enabled collaboration tools connect distributed teams and facilitate effective remote work. Environmental responsibility initiatives demonstrate commitment to sustainability and attract environmentally conscious talent

Organizational Response Requirements

To meet these challenges, organizations must implement comprehensive strategies across multiple dimensions. They need to develop comprehensive leadership development strategies that build capabilities at all organizational levels. Creating adaptive learning environments enables continuous skill development and knowledge sharing. Implementing flexible work policies accommodates diverse employee needs while maintaining productivity. Fostering inclusive culture ensures all perspectives are valued and leveraged. Balancing automation with human touch preserves the essential human elements of work while capturing technological efficiencies. Maintaining ethical business practices builds trust with all stakeholders.

Market Positioning

Companies must position themselves strategically through several key mechanisms. A clear value proposition to diverse stakeholders articulates the unique benefits the organization offers to different groups. Strong employer branding attracts and retains top talent in competitive markets. Sustainable business practices demonstrate long-term thinking and responsible resource management. Technological leadership establishes competitive advantage through innovation and digital capabilities. Social responsibility initiatives connect organizational success to broader societal wellbeing.

This evolving status quo requires organizations to fundamentally rethink their approach to leadership and organizational agility. Success depends on the ability to integrate these various elements while maintaining operational effectiveness and competitive advantage.

1.1 Demography

Demography is becoming increasingly important from the point of view of "demographic change". This term refers to the development of the population. In particular, changes in the birth and death rate are of great importance. Demographic data also includes people moving in and out of a country. In Germany, demographic change has played a major role since 1970 because the death rate is increasingly lower than the birth rate (bpb 2022).

In the search for talent, companies are facing major challenges due to demographic change. In order to overcome them, it is essential to keep an eye out for diverse employees. Areas requiring specialist knowledge in particular will become increasingly difficult to fill in the coming decades. The labor market is one of the major areas of society in which serious measures are needed to maintain economic efficiency and prosperity.

Demographic change is widespread throughout Europe and its effects are already being felt. Although there are countries within the European Union where the population is forecast to grow, there are also many members where the population will decrease.

The working population is shrinking. Life expectancy is increasing because people's health disposition and medical care are better than they have ever been in the past. Some people are able and willing to work longer than the normal retirement age.

At the same time, the proportion of older people is increasing, some of whom are living many years beyond retirement age, which increases the need for nursing and care facilities.

Rural areas are suffering the most from demographic change. In terms of the labor market, it is to be feared that there are talented people who remain in their home country but are unable to find adequate work. A lack of transport infrastructure exacerbates the problem.

The biggest problem is that the population is shrinking and the ratio of older to younger people is shifting drastically. Overall, the number of older citizens in Europe will increase. Between 2011 and 2021, the 15-29 age group decreased from 18.1% to 16.3%. This trend is unstoppable and will intensify, especially in rural regions. While 20% of the European population is older than 65 today (2023), this figure is expected to rise to around 30% in 2050.

The percentage of Europe's population in relation to the world's population is also decreasing. While it is still 6% today, only 4% is expected by 2070. This means that Europe, and the European Union in particular, will lose global significance if the trend continues. This will also have consequences for companies. Efforts to attract diverse talent will have to be stepped up significantly.

The situation in Germany is no better than the average in Europe. The decline in the birth rate is linked to the ageing population. It fell by 5.6% in 2022, measured against the average rate for the years 2019 to 2021. This corresponded to 739,000 newborns. A low level was also recorded in the first three months of 2023, in which 162,000 children were born. (Federal Statistical Office 2023)

The baby boomers will be around 80 years old between 2039 and 2050. This means that the number of very old people will reach a new record high. In 2018, there were around 5.4 million people aged 80 and over living in Germany. In 2050, there will be between 8.9 and 10.4 million. This means that the age structure is increasingly shifting towards a socially and economically problematic imbalance between working and non-working people. This is because the number of members of the next generation is declining. This is a predictable factor, as the maximum number of women who can give birth is known. Potential mothers are between 15 and 45 years old.

The birth rate in 2022 was 1.36 children per German woman. This was a decrease of 9% compared to the same year in 2021 with 1.49 children. For foreign women, the rate fell by 6% to 1.88 children in 2022, compared to 2.01 children in 2021. Statistically, however, a woman would have to give birth to 2.1 children to keep the population at a constant level.

At the same time, the population is very likely to decrease systematically (unless some of the factors that led to the statistical survey change significantly, such as the birth rate or the number of immigrants). While it will be around 83 million in 2035, it is assumed to be around 78 million in 2060 (bpb 2022).

At the same time, employees are placing demands on working conditions and demanding co-determination, participation and freedom. This is very evident in flexible working, which emerged during the pandemic and is now an integral part of many people's working reality and should remain so. In 2020, one in five employees worked from home. In 2019, it was still one in seven (commission.europa 2023).

As things stand today, the challenge of demographic change in Europe and Germany will not be overcome without immigration and, in particular, without the inclusion of diverse people. In this respect, it is not only socially but also economically important for companies to make an effort to recruit diverse talent. This applies not only to large companies, but also to small and medium-sized enterprises.

1.2 Fundamental development trends

1.2.1 Automation

The market is placing ever greater demands on companies. On the one hand, this is a consequence of globalization, which is connecting more and more companies around the world. On the other hand, it is also due to technological progress. It has led to an enormous acceleration in production and communication processes. Services are also expected at an ever faster pace.

The pressure to establish new products or services in the economic process is increasing accordingly. From development to placement on the market (time-to-market), months to years must be planned. As this time is becoming shorter and shorter in order to achieve efficiency, managers are reliant on a wide range of talent. A company's competitiveness is crucially dependent on having a competent and motivated workforce at all levels.

Multiple qualifications are in demand. Companies need more and more employees who are suited to current and long-term factors. In addition to conserving resources and respecting sustainability, this includes automation. It is the basis for process optimization. This, in turn, is based on good data analysis, which requires appropriate IT expertise. An American study found that more than half of companies are looking to automate their processes (deloitte 2023). In addition, companies must expect unforeseeable events at any time, to which they must react quickly. One example is the disruption to supply chains, which has had devastating consequences for both consumers and companies as a result of the Covid 19 pandemic.

These factors alone indicate that Hyper Leadership is playing an increasingly important role in the workforce of twenty-first century organizations.

One of the most important factors in automation is robot-assisted process automation, or RPA for short. Here, software robots (known as BOTs) learn and automate certain types of activities. These are repetitive, manual, time-consuming and error-prone tasks (Czarnecki 2018).

However, automation must be scalable so that the operating processes can be carried out. Scalability means that an electronic system (hardware and software) can increase its performance when resources (e.g. additional hardware) are added.

The increase must be correct, i.e. either linear or proportional (Wikipedia Scalability 2024).

The global company Automation Anywhere commissioned a study to identify the requirements of automation and scalability. The research team behind the "Making Work Human" study came from the University of London. The results included the following (Automation 2019).

1. Corporate culture

With the new technological requirements brought about by automation, the corporate culture must also evolve. Short-term applications in the field of automation are not sufficient for fundamental changes. Long-term planning and systematic change are required. This applies not only to operational processes, but also to the entire corporate attitude, which is reflected at all levels. The new corporate culture must be consciously defined, made transparent and practiced.

2. Competencies

Automation affects every workplace sooner or later. This means that employees must be behind the change processes. They must be given the appropriate skills to do so. A short-term changeover will not ensure efficiency in the long term if employees are not behind it or if they are overwhelmed.

3. Authenticity

The advancement of technological innovations should be kept within manageable limits in order to maintain employees' trust in the company. Operational processes should remain transparent. A sudden radical change does not pay off in the long term. Change processes affect employees, so it is important that they are also supported by them.

4. Resilience

Both management and employees need the courage to embrace change. Automation is a development process in which new skills must be learned in order to be able to use them.

5. Gender neutrality

Confidence in automation processes is necessary for both female and male employees. Care should therefore be taken to use new technologies in a gender-neutral way.

The study also found that well-managed automation in companies makes work more humane. A comparison showed that companies that use digital workers were rated a third better in terms of greater humanity in the world of work.

Point 5 of the study already shows that companies should focus on their female employees in order to keep up with the changes in the world of work. The proportion of women among technology professionals is low, e.g. only 22 percent of global IT experts are female.

But there is another necessity. All diverse people must also be involved in change processes. They cannot succeed without their help. This is now not only a moral but also an economic requirement for a society that is facing radical innovations.

1.1.2 Knowledge society

The term "knowledge society" has become established. A knowledge society is taken for granted in the highly industrialized economies of the world. But what does this mean in concrete terms?

The sociological term states that the factors of knowledge and competence play a central role for growth in modern (i.e. highly industrialized) societies. Knowledge is, so to speak, a raw material that economic processes cannot do without. This implies that necessary knowledge that is not available ad hoc must and can be procured in the shortest possible time. This applies to collective knowledge as well as individual knowledge (Politlexikon 2020).

A company must therefore not only ensure that the management level has sufficient knowledge to maintain and further develop productivity and efficiency; it must also ensure that all employees have access to knowledge and can apply it optimally.

It is already clear here how differentiated the workforce of the future must be in order to be able to apply this knowledge at all levels. This means, among other things, that the cooperation of diverse employees will become increasingly necessary, both in terms of quantity and quality.

Knowledge and education are linked. Alongside capital, they are becoming increasingly important production factors. While innovations used to be the result of individual inventiveness and scientific research, knowledge is now required at every stage of most economic processes. The workforce itself is involved. This applies above all, but not only, to the use of technological instruments.

It is already clear here that not all employees have the knowledge currently required. Continuing professional development and training will therefore become increasingly important. A company is increasingly becoming a learning system. However, this will not only be necessary in terms of content, but also in terms of achieving an appropriate level of knowledge throughout the workforce in the area of leadership.

Achieving this is facilitated by the fact that a general change in the work process is to be expected. Where previously, in many areas, fixed tasks had to be carried out, today far more creativity and independence is required. The knowledge society requires less obedient execution of instructions and more assumption of responsibility by employees, both for the execution of their work and for the results (Knowledge Society 2024).

The application of knowledge is essential, but employees need to develop new skills at the same time. A study from the field of HR management shows that this also includes social skills (Diversity Charter 2024). This is not least due to the fact that more and more people from different stages of life and with different values need to be included. As part of the expansion of knowledge and skills, companies should therefore also promote greater openness to diversity.

The American author Richard Florida argued as early as 2002 that the USA is on the way from an industrial to a knowledge society. In his book "The Rise OF The Creative Class", he explains that this transition is producing a wide variety of different lifestyles and working styles. The organizational consultant and political scientist Andreas Merx reports on his findings (Merx 2006). Florida refers to the development of metropolitan areas. His ideas have since been adopted in various places in Germany. This is not surprising insofar as it can be assumed that the developments he describes will follow with a time lag in Germany.

Florida proclaims a fundamental structural change for urban life. This includes companies and, in turn, service companies. For him, the labor market will change dramatically and companies will have to adapt.

He sees knowledge as the basis for success because new ideas offer an advantage in the globalized economy. The second decisive factor for him is creativity. He identifies both as relevant growth resources and productive forces of the future. This leads him to the conclusion that Hyper Leadership will play an increasingly important role. His reasoning is as follows.

Creative and innovative thinking and action require a climate of openness to new ideas in order to flourish. This means that influences other than the usual ones are also accepted. People who think differently are welcome in such an environment. Creative solutions emerge where the exchange of knowledge is practiced openly and intensively. As a result, very different perspectives and skills are incorporated. This in turn happens when people of different ethnicities and cultures work together. Different ways of living and working prove to be fruitful for successful innovative processes.

Florida points out that social skills such as tolerance and mutual recognition form the basis for these processes. He calls for a non-discriminatory climate in which individuality is respected (Florida 2014).

These considerations can be applied to future-oriented companies. It is about allowing inspiration in a knowledge society that would not be possible without leadership. Integration is not enough. Integration means accepting a small group as a group within a larger group. This outdated perspective should be replaced with one centering around inclusion: every individual in every group must be recognized and valued for who they are. Companies need to implement this social task in the operational context.

1.1.3 Technology, outsourcing and partnering

There is often a fear that technology could jeopardize jobs. There are conflicting views and assessments as to whether enough new jobs will be created if technological processes replace human labor.

However, it is clear that technical innovations are increasing the number of employable workers with regard to diverse people. Assistance systems make it possible for people with disabilities to be gainfully employed. For a long time, this was not possible for them. Instead of being able to take on a normal job, they were often more or less shunted off to workshops for people with disabilities. Language programs also help with communication in everyday working life. This makes it possible to employ staff with different native languages.

Small and medium-sized companies that will no longer be able to hold their own on the market in the near future without digital technology should also expressly face up to such considerations.

Nowadays, the IT sector in particular offers the opportunity to outsource. Specialized services and tasks that lie outside the core business can be outsourced here. This outsourcing reduces the need for internal specialists, which also means a reduction in costs.

IT outsourcing means that you have a better chance of finding workers. This is partly due to the fact that diverse people are also deployed here. Geographical boundaries are easily overcome. Outsourcing partner companies in particular often have well-established leadership programs and a correspondingly diverse talent pool.

IT outsourcing allows companies to benefit from the flexibility and resources of partner companies. Their own problems of not being able to meet some of the needs of their own employees are solved here. For example, there are often difficulties in reconciling work and private life. It helps enormously when several companies join forces so that they can achieve a synergy effect in terms of working hours. Partner companies also often offer a supportive working environment in order to promote a diverse workforce. This improves a company's reputation among its customers, who come from a wide variety of backgrounds. Working with diverse people generally creates a competitive advantage.

Outsourcing partner companies also often provide training programs for their employees, including those that promote intercultural skills. IT outsourcing helps to build a global talent pool. By working with diverse people, a large amount of knowledge, skills and cultural perspectives are accumulated. This fulfills a good part of the requirements for innovation that a knowledge society needs.

Another effect is that you keep pace with the latest IT developments, which quickly gives you an advantage over competing companies. In addition, the partner companies bear part of the risk. Operational disruptions are also minimized.

Small companies and start-ups should also consider IT outsourcing and thus the involvement of diverse workforces, as they often find it difficult to set up their own IT department. However, IT is indispensable in the long term. It is increasingly becoming an integral part of everything from personnel planning to online training (Medium 2023).

In addition to outsourcing, partnering is playing an increasingly important role. This approach is already being pursued in the construction and real estate industries in particular.

Partnering is a management approach used by two or more organizations to achieve specific business goals. The approach is based on common goals. Cooperation is intended to increase the effectiveness of all participants and conserve resources. The methods to be used for joint problem solving are defined in joint agreements. The results should be measurable (Core 2016).

Any company can enter into partnering arrangements with external partner companies. The basic components are the agreement of targets, procedures and the way in which decisions are made. The basic aim is to improve economic success. To date, there is no clear, standardized business definition of partnering. (Soldan 2023). However, as the construction and real estate sector has already gained experience in this area, it is important for other sectors to learn from it.

The latest technology came into the world with artificial intelligence and is increasingly influencing operational processes. It will continue to develop and expand. It is undoubtedly one of the factors that is profoundly changing the structure of work. Its impact goes beyond what automation has already achieved. This transformation is being driven by the fact that far-reaching networks already exist. Artificial intelligence can act independently, incorporate experience and communicate with people. Here, too, there are fears at a societal level that entire jobs will be lost, while at the same time there is hope that just as many new ones will be created.

The American scientist David Autor and others investigated which new professions were created in the course of automation. The study found that 60 percent of today's workforce is employed in jobs that did not exist in 1940. (National Bureau of Economic Research 2022). In this respect, it can be assumed that this process will also continue with regard to artificial intelligence.

Artificial intelligence has not yet been definitively defined. It is associated with the fact that machines use intelligence to accomplish a wide range of tasks and even learn. However, this raises the questions of how intelligence should be defined, whether machines can be intelligent at all and, if so, how this differs from human intelligence.

So far (2023), it is mainly large companies that are using artificial intelligence to advance automation. For many medium-sized and initially quite small companies, the question of weighing up the costs and benefits arises. A study by the Federal Ministry for Economic Affairs and Energy found that less than 6% of German companies were using artificial intelligence by 2019. Of these, it was only a key component of the business model for 12%. It is used in a variety of ways, from product development, marketing and customer service to personnel monitoring. At the same time, however, it is clear that jobs that use artificial intelligence cannot be filled due to a lack of skilled workers (Bundeszentrale für politische Bildung 2023).

This in turn reflects the influence of the knowledge society, which brings its own structures and challenges, as well as the need to recruit a more diverse workforce.

1.2 Changing employee expectations

1.2.1 Values and Corporate Purpose

In the changing world of work, it is important for companies to align their own values with those of their employees. As people who want to be employed seek meaningful and purpose-driven work, it is crucial for managers to respond effectively.

Corporate purpose and values must increasingly go hand in hand. Today's workforce is aware of where they work and what they work for. It matters what their company stands for. It should not only make a profit - to pay salaries, of course - but also make a meaningful contribution to society. For many, it also makes a difference whether or not supplier companies have their production in countries where the minimum requirements for humane working conditions apply. Who works where and why is increasingly being questioned in everyday conversations, not least in connection with issues of leadership.

When employees can identify with the values and purpose of the company, their commitment to their work increases. They have the conviction that their individual work at their workplace has meaning and is an important contribution beyond value creation. They do not have to separate their professional activity from their private life in terms of their personal beliefs. They are therefore much more willing to adapt to changing conditions.

Employees' values are increasingly determined by the fact that they can live their individuality. In the age of social media, everyone can get involved. At the same time, skilled workers are being sought, which means that specialized knowledge is in demand. The more individual your own ideas are allowed to be without being judged, the more leadership will be accepted.

For companies, this means that their opportunities to find and retain talent are expanding. Diverse people are more confident and find more courage to apply for a wide range of jobs. However, paying lip service to leadership does not help. All talents are needed and retaining them is an essential part of long-term success. This is why it is not only important at a social level and in public life to help diverse people achieve inclusion, but also in business. Companies must create a corporate structure and atmosphere in which they can increase their added value by treating all employees with respect.

There are already companies that have not only taken up the cause of innovative values, but are also pursuing them. Here are some examples of large companies that operate internationally (Together 2023).

The toy company Mattel is working to increase the proportion of women and members of different ethnic groups. It is also committed to paying equal pay for equal work.

The consultancy firm KPMG wants to increase underrepresented groups at management level to 50%. The focus here is on doubling the proportion of people with black skin. This proportion is also to be increased in all management positions as well as in client circles.

McDonald's (fast food restaurants) has set itself the goal of increasing the proportion of underrepresented groups in the management of US companies. By 2025, at least 35% of management positions are to be filled by people who have historically been underrepresented for a long time. After that, a further increase to 45% is targeted. Salary payments are to be regularly reviewed in parallel. The principles of Hyper Leadership should apply. The company intends to provide training to this end.

In 2022, the software company Salesforce already had a 50% share of women in its workforce. In 2023, the proportion of underrepresented groups in management positions was doubled. At its US headquarters, Salesforce increased the proportion of African-American and Latin American employees to 50 %. It pursues equality in teams, at management level and in the operational environment.

The software company Adobe has set itself the goal of increasing the proportion of women in management positions worldwide to 30% by 2025. It has also entered into partnerships with colleges and universities that traditionally educate people of color. In this way, Adobe wants to encourage more graduates from these institutions to apply for jobs at its company.

In 2020, Hershey, one of the world's largest chocolate manufacturers, launched the "Pathways Project" together with employees to create a diverse and inclusive workplace. (Thehersheycompany 2024). As part of this, it also created new recruitment guidelines. They state that new paths must be taken to find talent. For example, it explicitly mentions African-American, Asian, Latin American, older, female and LGBTQ+ people. In addition, at least 50% of the personnel management in the job interviews should consist of diverse employees in order to ensure a fair assessment of each applicant.

One example of a German company is Dieter Albrecht Henkel AG. The listed company in the consumer goods and adhesives industry with global brands and technologies defined innovative guidelines for its corporate purpose in the 2010s. These include a commitment to leadership. Henkel emphasizes that it promotes the leadership of its employees and employs people from many cultures. The company points out that the experience, knowledge and creativity of its diverse workforce are the basis for its competitiveness. In this context, Henkel sees its commitment to sustainability. It also acknowledges its responsibility for health and quality of life not only for its customers, but also for its employees.

Henkel has created the "Sustainability at Heart" program specifically for committed employees. This is an interactive platform that offers a central point of contact with a wide range of tools. It pursues three main objectives, namely providing up-to-date information and materials, offering various training formats and networking opportunities (Henkel 2024 , Silo 2016).

This example shows how strongly openness to leadership is linked to a commitment to sustainability. Both require open-minded, non-discriminatory, objective and innovative thinking.

1.2.2 Understanding of work

Today's employees are attaching more and more importance to a good work-life balance, and it is not only the compatibility of work and family that plays a role. There is also an increasing focus on leisure activities, including requests for a sabbatical year. Even here it is clear that companies are being called upon to act. Offers ranging from flexible working hours to sports facilities need to be considered.

But there must be factors that originally motivate people to work. This was investigated by management consultants Deloitte (Deloitte 2024). In 2018, one of the priorities in Germany was that the job itself should be seen as secure.

Employees considered their salary to be equally important. This was in line with the European trend. However, people in employment were not more satisfied if they were paid better compared to other companies, while they were significantly less satisfied if they received a lower salary.

The German employees also stated that, in addition to the meaningfulness of their work, they attached importance to clear responsibilities and an atmosphere of trust. For older employees, content and complex issues were important, while younger employees were concerned about how they were supported by colleagues and management.

These results show the different challenges facing today's companies. At the same time, many workplaces are undergoing radical changes. This means that employees must also face up to this process and be prepared to continue learning. While 53% across Europe stated that they needed to improve their learning skills, only 43% in Germany did so.

What about employees' fear of being replaced by automation and artificial intelligence? The global "Making Work Human" study from 2019, initiated by Automation Anywhere, provided some insights (Automation 2019). According to the study, 73% of the 4,000 employees surveyed did not believe that technology would replace them. Rather, they believed that jobs would be retained and technology would be integrated. Two thirds wanted to learn more about how modern technologies can make work processes easier.

As of 2019, 38% of respondents were already using technology in the workplace. Across the world, employees' acceptance of such innovations obviously varies. Although there was widespread agreement that automation and artificial intelligence would increase productivity, 13% of Japanese and 26% of British workers wanted to avoid using them - compared to 49% of US and 66% of Indian workers who welcomed them as a relief.

How are managers adapting to the new challenges? Deloitte conducted the global study "Human Capital Trends 2023" (Deloitte 2023) to find out. 59% of respondents stated that they see the redesign of workplaces as a priority in the years 2024 to 2028.

New technologies not only play a major role in operational areas and administration, they also have an impact on virtually all workplaces. Entrenched divisions of workplaces must therefore be broken, and not just for purely economic reasons. This should also make life easier for employees. The dissolution of the traditionally fixed workplace was practiced to some extent during the Covid pandemic between 2020 and 2022. This process should be driven forward. From a physical and digital perspective, employees need an environment that meets their different personal dispositions, needs and requirements. However, only 22% of the managers surveyed stated that their company had already prepared for such changes. At the same time, 93% felt that they needed to move away from conventional definitions of how work should be done. 33% said they were unable to find enough talent to meet the current demands of their business.

This again highlights the need to involve diverse people more, and to do so in reality and not just as a commitment on paper. Seeking out diverse talent, guaranteeing them a fair application process and including them successfully is not something that can be achieved in a short time and without a concept. In Germany, for example, there is a discrepancy between public commitment and actual implementation. According to statistical data, 82% of companies include diversity in theory, while only 44% actively address it in practice (pens.com 2024).

In highly industrialized Germany, the largest economy in Europe in terms of gross domestic product and the third largest economy, women must be counted among the diverse workforce in terms of their presence in management positions (Wikipedia 2024). At the same time, there is a shortage of skilled workers at all levels in SMEs and family businesses. Despite legal requirements and social pressure, it has not yet been possible to appoint female managers to higher positions.

A recent study by HR consultancy Stanton Chase Stuttgart GmbH and the Aalen Institute for Corporate Management at Aalen University has investigated possible causes and found results with regard to gender-specific differences in the understanding of work (Jot 2022). According to the study, the requirements for managers should be better adapted to the - partly gender-specific - needs of applicants. Men and women place equal value on opportunities to shape the company, a comprehensible vision of the company's future, opportunities for personal development, flexibility and a satisfactory salary. Today, managers of both genders in medium-sized companies want to be involved in the company, for example through shares in the company.

However, men attach great importance to shareholdings, as well as to a good salary and material benefits (e.g. a company car), while for women the values of family friendliness, a sense of purpose within the company's mission and a good work-life balance are important. Medium-sized companies in particular could use their values and visions to get more women on board. Among other things, they would have to work on formulating their job advertisements more specifically so that women feel better addressed (Jot 2022).

1.2.3 Qualification profile

The competitiveness of companies is closely linked to the qualifications of their employees. This means that the workforce must be adequate in terms of both quantity and quality. This is not easy to achieve. Outsourcing and partnering can help here. This has already been explained with regard to IT. But it also applies to other areas. The Covid crisis has strengthened and promoted the ability of employees to work from home. Both employees and employers have developed noticeably. Both sides have recognized the benefits of working from home. You don't need in-depth IT knowledge to do this. But you can share knowledge and results globally.

With regard to the qualifications that a company needs but cannot fully provide itself, it is worthwhile establishing cooperation and partnerships with other companies from the same sector. Joint ventures lead to the sharing of resources and mutual support. If a specific skills profile is required that not every HR management can provide, various working models can be used to remedy the situation. For example, sharing research and development work can help accelerate innovation and time to market. Start-ups should not be neglected in the search for partnerships. It is often with them that expertise can be found.

Today's companies are re-evaluating qualification profiles in several areas. This is necessary because there is a shortage of skilled workers and at the same time the knowledge society is advancing. Expertise is often even required in niche areas. At the same time, employees are needed to fill the knowledge gaps between different areas, e.g. in the healthcare sector, not only knowledge of health factors is needed, but also extensive technological knowledge.

This process of change towards innovative and differentiated requirements and measures can only work if employees are willing to learn. There is not a suitable person for every specified job. This is partly because such employees are rare on the labor market and partly because the specification is not necessarily a requirement that is already demanded in a job description.

A large area of the skills required has arisen from the digital transformation. For the foreseeable future, employees with skills in data analysis, artificial intelligence, cyber security and digital marketing will be needed. This ongoing development requires constant adaptation to new findings and new technologies. However, many other jobs are also affected whose core process does not involve these technologies, but where they are used. Almost every type of device is being digitized. Even if the application itself is simple, it needs to be learned. Many people who have been used to a different method of operation for years find the new method difficult.

This development requires a fundamental willingness on the part of employees. A global study has shown how they react to change. As part of a global talent survey conducted together with the Boston Consulting Group and The Network, a total of 208,807 people were surveyed between October and early December 2020 (Stepstone 2021). The results show that 70% of employees were willing to retrain or take on a new role at work. 65% had undertaken further training measures a year previously.

It was generally evident that people with a higher level of education were more willing to regularly update and expand their knowledge. However, there were differences in terms of origin. It emerged that people in African countries spend the most time on further training measures worldwide. European and US employees were at the bottom of the statistics. In addition, African people show the greatest tendency to change their area of specialization. At the same time, there are fewer highly qualified people in Africa.

This shows how important Hyper Leadership is in companies. According to this survey, simply increasing the proportion of employees from African countries would increase the chances of attracting committed employees. Any lower qualifications are likely to be well compensated for by the great willingness to continue learning. This opportunity for personnel management does not even take into account other diverse people.

However, specialist knowledge and a willingness to expand current knowledge appropriately are not the only qualifications that are important in order to hold your own on the market in the long term. You also need to have the right personality traits. Above all, a strong ability to work in a team is important. Problem-solving processes increasingly require several people with different qualifications to work together. A brilliant person who has the decisive idea is becoming increasingly unlikely as a problem solver. On the other hand, the fundamental ability to solve problems is increasingly in demand. This requires a clear analytical view as well as the willingness to recognize when someone else makes a good contribution. This is why good communication skills are also an indispensable qualification in several operational areas.

However, there is a need for action here. This is because employees have a tendency to overestimate their personal qualities. In the survey, for example, 60% of Germans thought they had good communication skills, compared to 48% across Europe. When it came to the ability to work in a team, the Germans scored 64%, compared to 57% across Europe. Both of these are skills that are difficult to self-assess. However, it is undeniable that employers should keep an eye on these skills. They should be prepared to provide further training to develop such skills.

The changes of our time mean that HR management needs to develop strategies and concepts that cover the following points (Bertelsmann Stiftung 2016):

- Fill vacancies with staff who have all or some of the qualifications that are important today.
- Plan for lifelong learning in employees' careers.
- Establish a corporate culture that promotes innovative thinking, teamwork and the sharing of personal knowledge.
- Create framework conditions that bind employees to the company, regardless of how long they have been with the company or their personal circumstances.

In order to meet these requirements, it is essential to involve diverse people in entrepreneurial activities.

Literature

bpb 2022, Federal Agency for Civic Education. Demographic change, accessed 28.05.2024, https://www.bpb.de/themen/soziale-lage/demografischer-wandel/

Federal Statistical Office 2023, Demographic change, accessed 28.05.2024, https://www.destatis.de/DE/Themen/Querschnitt/Demografischer-Wandel/_inhalt.html

commission.europa 2023, Impact of demographic change, in Europe, accessed 28.05.2024, https://commission.europa.eu/strategy-and-policy/priorities-2019-2024/new-push-european-democracy/impact-demographic-change-europe_de

deloitte 2023, Tech Trends 2024, accessed 28.05.2024,
https://www2.deloitte.com/us/en/insights/focus/human-capital-trends.html

Christian Czarnecki, Gunnar Auth: Process digitization through robotic process
automation. In: Digitization in companies: From Theoretical Approaches to Practical
Implementation (= Angewandte Wirtschaftsinformatik). Springer Fachmedien
Wiesbaden, Wiesbaden 2018

Automation 2019, New study: Employees are not afraid of being replaced by AI and
automation, accessed 28.05.2024,
https://www.automationanywhere.com/de/company/press-room/new-study-employees-
are-not-afraid-to-be-replaced-by-ai-and-automation

Wikipedia Scalability 2024, Scalability, accessed 28.05.2024,
https://de.wikipedia.org/wiki/Skalierbarkeit2. Knowledge society

Florida, Richard: The Rise of the Creative Class Revisited, 2014

Political lexicon 2020, Knowledge society, accessed 28.05.2024,
https://www.bpb.de/kurz-knapp/lexika/politiklexikon/296549/wissensgesellschaft/

Knowledge society 2024, An idea in a reality check 2013, accessed 28.05.2024,
https://www.bpb.de/themen/bildung/dossier-bildung/146199/wissensgesellschaft-eine-
idee-im-realitaetscheck/

Diversity Charter 2024, Digitalization - Everything is changing, accessed
28.05.2024, https://www.charta-der-vielfalt.de/fuer-arbeitgebende/arbeitswelt-im-
wandel/digitalisierung/

Merx 2006, Location factors tolerance and diversity by Andreas Merx, retrieved
28.05.2024, https://www.idm-diversity.org/deu/infothek_merx-standortfaktor.html

Medium 2023, The Benefits of IT Outsourcing for Fostering a Diverse and Inclusive
Workforce, accessed 28.05.2024, https://medium.com/@livajorge7/the-benefits-of-it-
outsourcing-for-fostering-a-diverse-and-inclusive-workforce-c2aaaf9b3db2

Federal Agency for Civic Education 2023 , Die Auswirkungen von Künstlicher
Intelligenz auf den Arbeitsmarkt, retrieved 28.05.2024,
https://www.bpb.de/themen/arbeit/arbeitsmarktpolitik/522513/die-auswirkungen-
von-kuenstlicher-intelligenz-auf-den-arbeitsmarkt/

National Bureau of Economic Research 2022, New Frontiers: The Origins and
Content of New Work, 1940-2018, accessed 28.05.2024,
https://www.nber.org/papers/w30389

Core 2016, Journal of Education and Practice2016, Vol.7, No.14, accessed 28.05.2024, https://core.ac.uk/download/pdf/234638985.pdf

Soldan 2023, Partnering as a management approach - definition and conceptual classification, accessed 28.05.2024, https://www.soldan.de/media/pdf/6b/c1/a5/9783170198616_LP.pdf

Silo 2016, Corporate Purpose, Vision, Mission, Values, Dieter Albrecht Henkel AG 2016, accessed May 28, 2024, https://silo.tips/download/unternehmenszweck-vision-mission-werte

Together 2023, DIVERSITY AND INCLUSION, accessed 28.05.2024, https://www.togetherplatform.com/blog/diversity-and-inclusion-performance-goals-examples

Thehersheycompany 2024, retrieved 28.05.2024, https://www.thehersheycompany.com/en_us/home/newsroom/blog/empowered-by-pathways-embarking-on-an-equitable-future-together.html#:~:text=The%20Pathways%20Project%20focuses%20on,more%20diverse%20and%20inclusive%20workplace.

Henkel 2024, OUR EMPLOYEES:INSIDE, accessed May 28, 2024, https://www.henkel.de/nachhaltigkeit/hebel-fuer-veraenderung/unsere-mitarbeiter-innen

Deloitte 2024, New world of work demanding, flexible and digital, accessed 28.05.2024, https://www2.deloitte.com/de/de/pages/human-capital/articles/neue-arbeitswelt-studie.html

Automation 2019, New study: Employees are not afraid of being replaced by AI and automation, accessed 28.05.2024, https://www.automationanywhere.com/de/company/press-room/new-study-employees-are-not-afraid-to-be-replaced-by-ai-and-automation

Deloitte 2023, Human Capital Trends 2023, accessed 28.05.2024, https://www2..com/de/de/pages/human-capital/articles/human-capital-trends-deutschland.html

Wikipedia 2024, Economy of Germany, retrieved 28.05.2024, https://de.wikipedia.org/wiki/Wirtschaft_Deutschlands

pens.com 2024, Status Quo: This is how diverse German companies are, accessed 28.05.2024, https://www.pens.com/de/blog/diversity-am-arbeitsplatz/

Jot 2022, Diversity management: pent-up demand in SMEs 2022, accessed 28.05.2024, https://www.jot-oberflaeche.de/branche/diversity-management-nachholbedarf-im-mittelstand-3188611.html

Stepstone 2021, Opportunities & risks of automation, accessed 28.05.2024, https://www.stepstone.de/e-recruiting/blog/chancen-risiken-der-automatisierung/

*Bertelsmann Stiftung 2016, Diversity Management and Work 4.0?, accessed 28.05.2024, https://www.zukunftdernachhaltigkeit.de/2016/07/15/diversity-management-und-arbeit-4-0-eine-andere-sichtweise-auf-eine-arbeitswelt-im-wandel-2/^*

2 The organization

Company management should create new forms of organization with flat hierarchies, team building and greater responsibility for employees. A strong focus on customers and employees is necessary. Automation and knowledge work must be incorporated in a forward-looking way. A corporate ethic should be clearly recognizable, including Hyper Leadership.

2.1 Why do we need a new form of organization?

In the globalized world, in which new challenges are constantly arising for every type of company, conventional forms of organization can no longer keep pace. This does not mean that we no longer need an organization, but rather that the organization should change. Haphazard action is still not called for.

There are various drivers that sooner or later make it clear to the management team that they need to adapt their organizational structure. These can be both expansion and downsizing processes. Operational processes that have been forced to change to a certain extent, for example because rationalization has become necessary, often result in an adjustment to the organization. It goes without saying that digitalization plays a major role in this. Changes are also often necessary because costs have risen disproportionately. Current reasons for this include the rise in energy costs (2023). Other current causes include a shortage of skilled workers and a shortage of resources, which in turn is often due to supply problems. There are also political and social reasons that affect the markets and whose development is sometimes difficult to predict.

Outdated or less future-oriented management structures can often be recognized by the fact that management is very preoccupied with itself. Many companies drop-down organizational charts often fail to mention their customers. They are characterized by a strong hierarchy and a strong tendency to conform. Linear assignments and traditional departments are predominant. This tends to turn employees into recipients of orders. There is little or no willingness to learn within the management team. However, innovative forms should be geared towards being a "place of longing" for customers and a "home port" for employees (Kundenorientierung 2017).

When making changes, it is not only necessary to structure along the lines of digitalization. Rather, the type of leadership and cooperation with and within the workforce must be taken into account. A new understanding of management is therefore required among managers. They are increasingly faced with the following developments:

- Changes are happening faster and faster, are becoming more frequent and more profound.
- Cooperation at all levels is becoming ever more complex and at the same time ever more necessary.
- The demands on knowledge and learning are becoming ever higher and in some cases more differentiated.

As a result, collaboration between different areas is becoming increasingly important. Interdisciplinary project work is increasingly defining working life and the need for virtual teams is growing. As a result, the organization needs to adapt. The following tasks arise

- the dismantling of hierarchical structures in favor of teams,
- the reduction of interfaces that exist within a department,
- the increased delegation of areas of responsibility to employees and
- Establishing an adaptable, resilient organization (consulting-btb 2024).

A heterogeneous workforce is necessary for the optimal realization of these points, which enables the development and maintenance of leadership. For management, this means bringing in new skills of their own. Social skills, empathy and a constant willingness to learn are required in order to adapt to diverse employees. An open mind in the best sense is the prerequisite for enabling economic growth. A management that does not at least consider new ideas and concepts sympathetically no longer has any chance of competing.

How could a restructuring process proceed? In principle, it should not be hierarchical and linear from top to bottom, by decree so to speak. Instead, all those involved should be informed at an early stage, taken along the entire way and involved as extensively as possible. An up-to-date analysis of the current situation is the starting point for any form of organization.

The following stations are useful (Con Cubo 2023):

1. Appoint responsible managers or employees for the restructuring process

A team is best. This team is also responsible for initiating the process. It must be determined which supporting people, positions, areas and factors will be involved. These include HR management and the works or staff council. Other areas need to be considered, such as risk management and quality management. It will hardly be possible to do without IT expertise.

2. Set clear goals

You need to determine precisely which changes are desired and necessary in order to position and assert yourself optimally on the market. Improvements should be precisely defined. If possible, you can operationalize this (break down goals into sub-goals) in order to gain an overview.

3. Present your current business model in its entirety

This requires a clear method. The so-called business model canvas is now an established method. Here, the overall business structure is divided into core areas. One option is to break it down into: core partnerships, core activities, core resources, value proposition, relationship with customers, channels to customers, customer segments, cost and revenue structure.

4. Model the processes

A distinction must be made between value-adding core processes and supporting processes. The value-adding processes must be subdivided into sub-processes in order to determine important factors such as resources, costs, risks, etc.

5. Present the organizational form visually

Visualizations are generally very useful for analyzing and understanding a situation. The usual organizational charts are inadequate here. It is no longer just about jobs and departments. It is much more about areas of responsibility and the capacities of individual employees.

6. Describe and categorize existing tools

This applies in particular to the IT structure and the software used, but also to all devices that are in use.

7. Explain the corporate culture

In this case, this does not refer to the external image, but to the values practiced in internal processes. In many cases, there are unreflected traditions that are passed on without change. In addition, management behavior and the type and scope of key figures should be presented here.

8. Identify risk factors

There are sore points in every form of organization that require special attention.

Now leadership comes into play. The role that leadership plays must be thoroughly understood. It therefore makes sense to include the category of leadership in the analysis. It is best to go through each point with this criterion in mind. Points 5 and 7 in particular play a key role in the inclusion of diverse people and a diverse culture. But you should also consciously focus on this factor in all other areas, because a new form of organization needs diverse people at almost all levels.

2.2 Customer obsession

Customer orientation is not a temporary necessity. It goes far beyond traditional customer service, which is often superficial. The focus is much more on the customer than it was in the past. Quite a few local physical stores have had to close because they have not yet gone through this learning process. Customer orientation has an impact on the organizational structure of the company because it is at the heart of the strategy. Some modern companies have even become "customer obsessed".

For an adequate, future-oriented customer focus, the entire company is required. The company guidelines already contain this point, which runs from the theoretical commitment through to the most differentiated level in the operational area. The entire workforce is convinced that customer satisfaction is not just a goal to be achieved in a current situation, but is a permanent shared responsibility that rests on all shoulders. It is part of the culture of a company.

The needs and preferences of customers are always at the forefront. On the one hand, this applies to the existing production chain or service offerings, but it also applies equally to the offerings that are to be developed. Companies therefore need close contact with their customers. This naturally applies to the existing target group. At the same time, it should not be neglected that this should be expanded. It is therefore always necessary to maintain an overview of the entire market at the same time.

Retaining customers is the top priority. This is becoming increasingly difficult in a globalized world with worldwide markets. Therefore, appropriate communication channels must be used at all levels. Developing new customer groups is not enough, even if they compensate for or even outperform possible migration processes to other companies. Maintaining the relationship is a decisive factor for long-term success. Without customer loyalty, a modern company cannot survive, let alone grow. Observing market trends in conjunction with customer evaluations forms an important basis for the necessary decisions relating to the development of new products.

Customer-oriented companies maintain continuous contact with their customers and value their feedback. It is precisely by incorporating feedback that they build trust, as this gives customers the feeling that their concerns are at the forefront and that they themselves are even initiating change processes in their favor. This results in brand loyalty among users, which in turn makes them advocates for the services to a certain extent. Customers behave loyally because they appreciate the company's behavior. This includes the fact that they can rely on the brands and look forward to innovations with confidence and enthusiasm.

How do you achieve optimum customer orientation? First of all, you need a well-functioning IT system. The customer support system must be stable and reliable. Availability day and night must be guaranteed. This requires chatbots that ensure the technical side of things. They have learning language processing so that they can constantly optimize their responses. This enables them to process even complex customer inquiries.

The second component is an online ticket system, especially for service companies. It ensures professional and systematic processing of inquiries from customers, but can also be used for dealing with suppliers. The system is easy to use - comparable to an e-mail system. It makes it possible to keep track of inquiries.

However, you also need the human component. It consists of optimally trained employees in terms of customer contact so that qualified support can be provided. This not only includes in-depth technical knowledge - very good rhetorical skills are also required here. Verbal communication that responds empathetically to the wishes, needs and comments of customers is essential. In particular, the ability to accept criticism in discussions with customers and not make judgments about what they say should be well developed - a skill that often has to be learned under professional guidance in a competitive society. Quick solutions to problems are often required, although "quick" is a word that cannot be dispensed with. At a time when society is experiencing an acceleration of processes in many respects, customers expect a short-term, if not immediate, solution to their concerns.

In addition to customer support channels, feedback tools are also important. These include surveys as well as social media activities and apps. Apps in particular allow for personal contact. Regular reporting with a personal salutation and current offers is an appealing communication tool.

People appreciate being treated individually or exclusively. This is especially true for customers who are prepared to invest money. Personalization is the magic word here. Meaningful data is important for this. Artificial intelligence is already being used for this purpose and will play an increasingly important role in the coming years. It offers the opportunity for personalized offers and can calculate forward-looking trends on the market.

One way to quickly and efficiently establish and strengthen the subjective customer experience is to use machine learning to generate up-to-date recommendations on a large scale. Amazon, for example, is working on this (Amazon 2023). Machine learning (ML for short) is the general term for the artificial generation of knowledge from experience. An intelligent system learns from examples and can generate generalizations from what it has learned. The system recognizes patterns and regularities from the data. Customers are served individually on the basis of this real-time data analysis. Incidentally, the ML method can also be used to detect credit card fraud and practice speech and text recognition (Wikipedia 2024).

Amazon is also a leader in applying a radical customer-oriented strategy for innovation, which has so far been very successful. In doing so, the company is abandoning the usual chronological approach to innovation. It no longer starts from what already exists, but works "backwards". Customers and their needs are at the beginning of the innovation process. This approach is called "working back" and offers a radical customer orientation.

As a starting point, the team drafts a fictitious press release. The content is the announcement of a new product that is being launched on the market. Due to the nature of the text, customer-oriented language must be used here. This means that even the most complicated product must be presented in a way that is easy to understand, otherwise neither the media will publish the press release nor will customers understand it straight away. This approach focuses on the needs of the customer. Only what is relevant to them becomes the basis for further planning and development.

This method takes into account the fact that around 30,000 new products flood onto the market every year, 95% of which fail (copetri 20213).

Leadership also plays a major role in customer orientation. There is an increasing need to focus on individual needs. It is therefore becoming increasingly important to take greater account of the starting points of diverse people and to respond to their wishes. At the same time, this requires diverse employees who have the relevant knowledge and the necessary empathy for specific innovations.

2.3 Employee obsession

The way in which employees are deployed in the company and how they are treated as individuals is undergoing a fundamental change in our time. The realization that employees play a central role in success is at the forefront. Just as important as focusing on the needs, interests and wishes of customers is the orientation towards the needs, perspectives and experiences of employees. This goes far beyond the question of who is assigned to which workplace. Even "the" workplace itself needs to be questioned, as flexibility and teamwork are playing an increasingly important role. Companies that see employees as mere workers and want to manage them optimally will no longer be able to keep up in the long term in a world of technological progress and increasingly dynamic and competitive markets. A modern management style as well as modern HR management takes into account the well-being of employees, who tackle their work every day not as an operational factor, but as a holistic human being.

Those who place a high value on employee orientation recognize that this is the only way to generate and sustain employee commitment. New employees are optimally integrated from day one so that they can identify with the values, mission and culture of their employer. To achieve this, each and every individual must feel recognized as an overall personality and feel that they belong.

The innovative company continuously offers measures for further training and individual development. Employees are given the opportunity to be deployed according to their skills, which they can also improve. They should be able to rely on the company to support their learning processes. As the business environment becomes increasingly dynamic, staff turnover processes are becoming a matter of course. However, because more and more teamwork is required at the same time, they are far less significant than in a rigid hierarchy.

Cross-functional collaboration on projects is an important part of employee orientation. In this way, everyone contributes their personal strengths and knowledge, which promotes creative solution strategies. At the same time, special individual achievements are recognized and rewarded. This can also involve contributing innovative ideas and suggestions. Employee orientation also means promoting personal involvement and encouraging a certain willingness to take risks. Breaking new ground is often necessary on the market.

In principle, good treatment of employees is based on transparent and open communication. Feedback is not only allowed, it is encouraged. At the same time, the company creates communication channels for employees, e.g. with platforms. The work culture is characterized by trust and team spirit.

Well thought-out and well-applied employee orientation saves personnel costs because it promotes employee loyalty to the company. In addition, employee satisfaction leads to customer satisfaction. Motivated employees are also good service staff. They are willing to adapt to changing conditions, both in terms of their working methods and their dealings with customers.

A pronounced employee orientation provides an environment in which diverse people feel comfortable because it creates an atmosphere in which the focus is on a common attitude for the good of the entire company, which results in the best for everyone involved in all areas. No person has to fear discrimination and can be confident that they are making an important contribution to the whole. It should therefore not matter what disposition someone was hired for. From career changers to highly specialized specialists, all employees should be valued equally.

Restricted stock units are an example of specific recognition measures for employees of stock corporations as an alternative to bonuses. They are a share-based variable remuneration element whose value usually depends on the market price of the company's shares. They are already widespread in the USA in particular. They offer a number of advantages. The loyalty of employees to the company is strengthened because there is a multi-year allocation plan for the shares. They also share in the overall success of the company. As they are taxed over several years, there are also tax advantages (Glns 2024).

However, modern employee orientation also means that management must be willing to learn continuously. This is not a common practice for everyone. Others simply lack knowledge about the effects of general progress on the world of work. It is therefore necessary to prepare new employees for this from the outset.

In a Europe-wide survey conducted in 2018, 80% of respondents stated that they expect slow, slight or no changes in their workplace over the next 10 years. 3 % assume that their job will be lost during this time. (Deloitte 2024) Many employees therefore still need to be convinced at management level. In principle, it is the responsibility of management to pick them up, and not the other way around.

In fact, many company managers have recognized that serious restructuring is necessary. In the "Human Capital Trends 2023" study, 10,000 managers from 139 countries provided information about their ability to change (Deloitte 2023). 93% stated that moving away from the conventional definition of "workplace" is relevant or very relevant to the success of their own company. This also means that work as a whole must be made pleasant for employees. This includes not only the opportunities to use technology, but also, for example, the provision of opportunities to do something for their health. The acceptance of leadership should also be mentioned here. 33% of respondents also stated that they could not find the right talent for their company.

2.4 Company organization

2.4.1 Company management

The management of a company includes management and leadership.

Many companies are dominated by traditional management, especially where there is a pronounced and differentiated hierarchy. To set innovative business processes in motion, you need management, but a future-oriented management level is just as important.

In the ever-evolving landscape of organizational success, the distinction between management and leadership has profound implications for attracting and retaining talent. While these two roles are linked, they serve different purposes within an organization.

Management is primarily about ensuring efficiency, control and order within an organization. Management employees are responsible for monitoring processes, resources and tasks in order to achieve predefined goals. Their focus is on executing plans, controlling budgets and maintaining stability.

Managers are often task-oriented. They are responsible for organizing and coordinating activities, allocating resources and measuring performance. Their success is often measured by how well they achieve the set objectives and maintain operational efficiency.

Management works within established hierarchies and relies on authority to ensure compliance with established rules and procedures. It exercises control to achieve defined objectives.

Leadership is about inspiring and motivating people to work towards a shared vision. Leaders are responsible for setting a compelling direction for the organization that inspires the commitment and enthusiasm of their teams.

Managers focus on people. They build relationships, promote talent and create an environment in which each individual can develop and reach their full potential. They know that motivated teams drive innovation and success.

Leadership is based on influence and trust, not authority. Leaders earn trust through their actions, their empathy and their authenticity. They set a good example and inspire others to follow them voluntarily and out of conviction, not out of a sense of duty.

While both management and leadership are critical to the success of an organization, leadership often proves critical to attracting and retaining top talent. Strong leadership inspires, empowers and creates an inclusive and growth-oriented culture that meets the demands of today's workforce. By recognizing the power of effective leadership, organizations can improve their ability to attract and retain the talent they need to succeed in a competitive and dynamic business environment. This talent fundamentally includes diverse people.

Effective leaders place a high value on the growth and development of their teams. They provide opportunities for skill building, mentoring and professional development. This commitment to personal and professional growth is a magnet for top talent looking for opportunities to learn and advance in their careers.

For these reasons, managers need a high level of social competence. Purely calculating factors that affect human resources does not lead to the goal. In fact, managers with a high level of emotional intelligence work most effectively. They can connect with their employees on a deeper level because they understand their needs and aspirations. Being able to empathize with them creates a sense of trust and psychological safety, which in turn promotes talent retention.

This management style adapts to the dynamics that prevail in economic and social processes. Both managers and employees must be able to act and think flexibly. On the other hand, there is also a growing need for harmony, which also seeks satisfaction in the workplace. Employers need to appeal not only to employees' minds, but also to their hearts.

The managers of the future will also have to face up to the advancing technological developments that are making the idea of a traditional workplace increasingly unfruitful. The collaboration of virtual teams will increase, this trend cannot be overlooked. This form of work is characterized by the following features:

- The members of the team are no longer physically in the same place. Rather, the physical workplaces can be far apart.
- A team works on a task for which a temporary limit applies. After that, the specific composition is likely to dissolve. New teams must be formed under new aspects.
- The members of the team can be interdisciplinary in order to achieve a common goal.
- Virtual teams need functional communication channels.

For managers, this way of working means that they should be in constant communication with the teams, including with the individual employees and not just with the team leaders. They must also ensure that the virtual teams always have all the necessary information at their disposal. Regular emails are hardly enough for this. Central information pools are needed, usually cloud-based ones. This can mean close cooperation with data protection officers.

Conventional forms of organization do not suit an innovative management style. The most far-reaching change in turning away from strict guidelines, authoritarianism and the need for control is exemplified by many start-ups. A new type of manager can be found here. Traditional superiors no longer exist. They are being replaced by employees who manage and lead projects and teams. Departments are organized across the board. Teams are authorized and tasked with achieving goals independently. This does not fit with a culture of instructions and guidelines. Instead, there are moderators and coaches. In such organizational forms, the areas of management and leadership even merge.

2.4.2 Automation for routine activities

It was long believed that automation would stand in the way of a humane working environment because employees would only have to operate buttons and levers. Not least through the use of artificial intelligence, it is becoming increasingly apparent that automation is leading to a general reduction in the workload in the world of work.

A company is fundamentally dependent on avoiding sources of error or identifying and eliminating them as quickly as possible, as well as increasing efficiency, productivity and competitiveness. All of this is no longer possible without automation. The Federal Agency for Civic Education drew attention to some research findings (bpb 2023). They included the finding that pioneering technological innovations have so far generated new employment opportunities and even new industries. For example, the Federal Ministry for Economic Affairs and Climate Protection found that a small amount of artificial intelligence created around 48,000 jobs between 2016 and 2018. In this respect, it can essentially be assumed that the workforce will not suffer from the use of automation.

As part of its own automation, a company should focus on rationalizing routine activities. This means that simple and recurring processes are affected. Many processes, especially if they relate to development, are not routine activities. Where creativity and innovative thinking are required, automation will not help. Automation, including the use of artificial intelligence, can qualitatively change part of the work, but cannot replace the work as a whole. Nevertheless, every company should monitor the automation processes used.

The pandemic in the early 2020s clearly demonstrated that automation can offer a major competitive advantage in routine activities, for example by enabling prioritization. But the need for this is fundamental. Medium-sized companies in particular are reluctant to introduce it. A simple example in the field of logistics shows how the use of a smart scheduling system for frequently requested goods can save a company costs and time (inform-software 2020):

- The system analyzes the order process and the development of sales.
- It calculates the best time for the next order process and indicates the quantity currently required.

- It generates a suggestion to place an order, which only needs to be confirmed by clicking on it.
- It shows various delivery conditions and service options.

The system generates the optimum use of goods by organizing and controlling the storage in the best possible way. It works far more error-free than human labor. In addition, taking over the entire order processing is easier because it is a multi-layered process in which different data records have to be reconciled. Automation saves time and resources here. Processes that are always repeated in a comparable manner are therefore generally candidates for use. The time saved can be used, for example, for the more intensive communication required by home offices and virtual teams.

These may not be surprising findings for large companies, as many things are already applied here. But in Germany, for example, just over half of the workforce is made up of small and medium-sized enterprises (Federal Statistical Office 2021). To ensure the survival of these companies, it is essential to consider automating routine activities. They secure operations from a technical perspective, but also in the interests of employees, whose work is made easier. Together with opening up to diverse employees, there is great potential here for the future in a world in which boundaries are dissolving on several levels.

One business model of the future is the disruptive business model - a typical product of the twenty-first century economy. Although the term disruptive literally means destructive, it should be considered by all company founders. It describes a model that leads to a leap innovation. It creates an unprecedented market. Conventional goods or services and even outdated technology are falling behind. One example is the internet giant Amazon, which has become the world's largest retailer without even owning any products. Another example is the ride-hailing service Uber, which has established itself in America. The company has understood that some of its customers are now less interested in cars as a commodity than in the "state" of being able to get around without their own car (Digitalzentrum-Chemnitz 2024).

Such radical market occupations are inconceivable without sophisticated automation processes. Among other things, they ensure that resources are used efficiently, creating synergy effects.

This requires an attitude that sees such processes not as a threat, but as an opportunity. This in turn requires a new form of organization and a modern idea of how employees should be recruited and managed, not to mention that leadership should be taken for granted.

The needs of customers are also at the forefront. A disruptive business model therefore always focuses on the current situation, combined with the perception, recognition and evaluation of a trend that will perpetuate itself. This in turn requires effective data processing based on the latest technology and the willingness to enter the business with a high level of automation.

2.4.3 Knowledge work

On closer inspection, today's knowledge society turns out to be a learning society, because knowledge develops at a rapid pace and has to be constantly adapted to ongoing processes. This is particularly true for organizations and companies.

Back in 2000, Martin Heidenreich from the Carl von Ossietzky University in Oldenburg drew attention to the contradictions that arise in companies as a result. He sees a serious moment on the social level in the differences between clearly hierarchical and largely non-hierarchical forms of organization. Every company must learn to deal with this area of tension. Hierarchy is intended to secure areas of responsibility, such as a well-functioning administration. This speaks in favor of departments. On the other hand, the initiative and motivation of employees should be encouraged, which satisfies the requirements of the knowledge society. This speaks in favor of group work as well as cross-departmental and interdisciplinary projects. Conflicts can now arise between specialist departments and the competencies of employees in individual projects. He illustrates this with the following example from a mechanical engineering company (Heidenreich 2020).

The company established a project group. This included sales staff and those responsible for design, production, sales and customer support. It turned out that the employees felt more responsible for the department they came from and its objectives than for the project. As a result, everyone tended to work on their own rather than together.

Other companies have also experienced this. They therefore strengthened the position of project managers. This created a different challenge, wherein the main managers lost contact with their own departments.

Heidenreich's comments show that employees identify with groups. Even if they identify with the company as a whole, they still tend to show a kind of solidarity with the area originally assigned to them. If they work in two areas (department and project), they therefore tend to prioritize.

Project work is integrated in many companies. However, the organizational form is not yet adapted to the knowledge society. Another pitfall with hierarchical forms of organization is that a new product is to be developed, but no cross-departmental team with different skills is working on it. Instead, two or more departments are involved. This creates competitive pressure. This blocks the urgently needed exchange of knowledge, even if product development itself is seen as a project.

In a knowledge society, knowledge must be available to everyone involved at all times. The appropriate communication channels must be available for this, but they must also be actively used. The importance of effective communication between employees is in no way inferior to that of customer service.

As a result, the responsibility for decisions shifts. It no longer lies with the divisional managers who allow employees to participate in the project, but with the project participants and, if necessary, the project management.

The knowledge society therefore requires agility as a form of work (greatplacetowork 2022). It means that companies can adapt to new situations and challenges as quickly as possible. Established structures are a hindrance to this. In an agile company, there are no rigid guidelines for a project. Instead, processes are constantly interrupted, evaluated and readjusted. Agile companies have flat hierarchies and are characterized by effectiveness and proactive action.

Critical thinking is encouraged at all times. The boundaries between the individual areas of the company are blurring. As a result, some areas are no longer clearly demarcated. Every new insight and every step forward is immediately communicated to the others.

This goes hand in hand with the fact that employees largely organize themselves in project work. The various experts work hand in hand. This even strengthens identification with the company, as employees identify with their project and its success. Procedures are not ordered but determined by agreement. Changes that are required by the company or the customer base can best be managed with well-run project work. It is the task of management to provide appropriate conditions for project work and to encourage employees in everything that supports this work.

An agile company is open to digital innovations because this is the best way to promote development and operational processes. In a knowledge society, companies therefore need both agility and digital transformation. Most companies are still on their way there, and only to the extent that they have recognized the innovative challenges. The Austrian management consultancy Great Place to Work has investigated the implementation of both factors. 1048 employees from Germany were surveyed. The result (greatplacetowork 2022):

43 % of employees were convinced that their employer would successfully manage the transformation.

52 % of managers believed that they would successfully overcome the problem.

58 % of the managing directors believed that they would be able to cope successfully.

The knowledge society requires rethinking and reorientation at a company level. This includes the leadership factor, and it fits very well into the new picture. The less hierarchy there is, the more company guidelines relate to the matter at hand and not to human attributes that have nothing to do with the matter at hand. The knowledge society shows that economic progress is only possible with progress in thinking that has freed itself from prejudices.

2.5 Corporate Purpose

2.5.1 Values

Corporate values are the values that a company represents. These are values that should apply both internally and externally. They form the basis for the corporate culture. This includes all rules, fundamental attitudes and lived habits that are defined or practiced in a company. If they are carefully selected and in line with the company's objectives, they have an impact on at least the following

- Selection and management of employees
- Selection of business partners
- internal processes such as new developments, e.g. of products

The applicable values should be known to the entire workforce. They help to ensure that work is perceived as meaningful and thus promote identification with the company. In this respect, they also have an impact on employee loyalty to the company. In return, employees can be expected to actively implement the values.

In principle, each company determines its own values. The most important of these include (Heidenberger 2023):

- Excellence (striving for the best quality)
- Cooperation
- Customer orientation
- Fairness
- Hyper Leadership
- Transparency
- Sense of responsibility
- Sustainability
- Independence Employee orientation
- Reliability

The multinational IKEA Group publicized the following values: modesty and willpower, leadership by example, courage to be different, togetherness and enthusiasm, cost awareness, willingness to innovate, and taking responsibility and delegating.

The international company Armacell International S. A. cited customer focus, employee focus, personal responsibility and accountability, integrity and sustainability.

Wolters Kluwer Deutschland GmbH has made innovation, customer focus, responsibility, integrity, value creation and teamwork its guiding values (Heidenberger 2023).

This small selection shows that the value of leadership is not yet firmly established everywhere. Although IKEA formulated (2023) "The courage to be different", this does not cover leadership comprehensively. Those who have the courage to be different do not necessarily have to be accepted. In contrast, leadership as a value not only means recognizing people's attributes, but also promoting inclusion - the natural inclusion of diverse people. This attitude is not only a humanitarian approach in the sense of respecting human rights, but must also be seen as essential for the realization of innovative corporate strategies.

The values of a company can be clearly seen when you look at the management style and how employees are treated. Of course, values also play a major role in dealing with customers. A company should always be able to justify its products and its behavior. Nevertheless, the focus here is on the market, as the company does not need to respond to the overall personality of a customer.

Although a conscious focus on values also serves to assert oneself on the market, the interpersonal component in the company-employee relationship cannot be overlooked. A company that does not respond to the dispositions and needs of its employees cannot expect authentic and therefore effective commitment. Those who identify with the company and its goals can expect to find a good working atmosphere and clear, open communication in return. This includes a feedback culture.

Especially in project work, a team assessment from time to time is essential for the good progress of the collaboration. The members should assess each other. This provides an overview of the team's overall performance. Team building is encouraged. However, professional guidance is recommended.

In a modern company organization, 360-degree feedback is a good idea. This includes self-assessment, assessment by superiors and assessment by team members (rexx-systems 2024).

Many companies have also installed a system in which line managers are assessed. Trust is the basis for the feedback that employees receive from their superiors. Trust is an irreplaceable human value in a company. Only on this basis can employees accept suggestions, observations and possible suggestions for change.

A company's values are not only reflected in written theses when dealing with employees. They are incorporated into daily work. Acceptance is a fundamental value that a modern company can no longer exclude if it wants to be successful. This includes Hyper Leadership. Appreciation, which implies communicated recognition, goes one step further.

The importance of applying theoretically defined values to practical activities can hardly be overestimated. If you want to create an agile company that is characterized by high adaptability, you have to take everyone who works in the company with you. To do this, you need to know their personalities and respond to them. Agility cannot be instructed, it has to be introduced empathetically. With the exception of start-ups that establish a modern form of company from the outset, many companies are faced with the task of implementing major change processes. A German study shows the extent to which employees are prepared to do this and highlights the reasons for this (greatplacetowork 2022).

There are several personality types that react differently to changing conditions depending on their individual disposition. There are essentially four types.

1. Active innovators

They enjoy facing change and complex challenges and think in a customer and solution-oriented way. They are enthusiastic about innovative business models. Such employees make up 9 % of the companies.

2. Optimistic employees

They are aware of the need for change and are confident about the future. They analyze the needs of customers and contribute to improving the business model. They can learn from mistakes and maintain open communication. 30% of such employees work in companies.

3. Stable employees

They trust in the existing business model, change is a burden for them. They do not want to share knowledge, but prefer to keep it as a power factor. 52 % of employees of this type are represented in companies.

4. Pessimistic employees

They experience change as threatening. Innovation makes no sense to them, nor does sharing knowledge. They are not committed to change and only comply with the most necessary requirements. These employees make up 10 % of employees in companies.

As these are average values, it must be assumed that a partial replacement of the workforce would not help. The company management is required to accommodate the individual types. This requires acceptance and communication. Outdated values such as a sense of authority and lack of independence run counter to change processes because they provoke employees to refuse to cooperate. What is needed is to strengthen a culture of trust and encourage employees to contribute their own ideas, offer constructive criticism and communicate without fear. This is supported not least by a pleasant environment. Employees who think innovatively and are optimistic must be integrated into the new processes in a skillful and supportive manner, and those who are stable and pessimistic must be taken along. All of this only works if the appropriate values are in place, including above all respect and appreciation for all employees.

Values that are communicated publicly also have an impact on the company's image and can therefore help to expand the customer base and strengthen competitiveness. The values flow seamlessly into the area of corporate ethics.

2.5.2 Business ethics

Business ethics overlaps with many values, but also goes beyond them in some respects. This applies above all to its external impact. This fact is explained by the fact that business ethics is part of business ethics. It is the guideline for both management and employees when it comes to the question of how ethically responsible decisions can be made. A company is caught between striving for economic efficiency and effectiveness on the one hand and its own demands to take moral values into account on the other. The aim is to achieve a good balance between the two.

Fundamental principles of corporate ethics are, for example, a sense of justice, responsibility, open communication and environmental awareness. What distinguishes the ethical principles from the canon of values is that they extend to the impact on society. Companies that act ethically assume social responsibility and commitment. Compliance with laws and regulations is a matter of course for them. Acting ethically is not compatible with fraud, corruption or overreaching. Ethical principles therefore shape the way we treat our employees, customers and business partners, as well as the needs and requirements of society and the environment. One of the positive aspects resulting from this is that companies that not only proclaim these principles but also act in accordance with them are less likely to become involved in legal disputes, for example in connection with fines.

A company's own corporate ethics often lead it to pursue corporate social responsibility (CSR for short). This refers to voluntary commitment to which a company is committed at a socially relevant level. This can be internal processes such as the avoidance of plastic products in the company, but often also measures such as participation in social community or regional projects. Companies can also engage in voluntary work and sponsorship. Naturally, these actions will have a public impact. This is one of the reasons why practicing corporate ethics also has an impact on the company's image. In particular, the qualities of reliability and trustworthiness are strengthened in the public perception through social commitment. A stable image in terms of corporate ethics also has a positive influence on economic stability (Homann 2023).

Tyco Fire & Security Holding Germany GmbH (which has since been merged into Johnson Controls), for example, showed how values and corporate ethics complement each other. It cited integrity, excellence, teamwork and responsibility as its guiding values. On this basis, she had launched corporate initiatives, including for health, prevention of risks to people and the environment, a network for women as well as diversity and inclusion (Heidenberger 2023).

Nowadays, not only customers but also employees judge a company by its ethical orientation. This trend is more likely to increase than decrease, as ethics include environmental protection, nature conservation and human rights, and these factors are increasingly appearing in the media and thus becoming more and more important to the general public. Potential employees are already looking at these points before applying for a job. Diversity is on its way to becoming one of these factors. However, as diverse people are usually a minority, this process must be actively supported (just like the promotion of women, who are not a minority in some companies).

In particular, the focus on respect for human rights is increasingly becoming the focus of public attention and is having an impact on the commitment of companies. In February 2024, the media reported that the pressure on Volkswagen AG to withdraw from its production site in the Chinese region of Xinjiang was growing. This was due to the fact that the chemical company BASF SE had announced its withdrawal at the beginning of February 2024. The reason was that employees of the partner company, Xinjiang Markor Chemical Industry, had spied on Uyghurs in the same region. BASF SE announced that this was not compatible with its values. In fact, on its website (2024), BASF SE states, among other things, the point "Responsible representation of interests" and writes: "We support and promote responsible, comprehensible, transparent and democratic processes that serve society as a whole." Volkswagen now found itself under pressure to draw the same conclusions (Merkur 2024, Zdf 2024, BASF 2024).

As ethical principles are increasingly becoming a socially relevant factor in companies, well-known personalities from business and science founded the Ethics Association of German Business in 2003. It has set itself the goal of "supporting companies and managers in adequately formulating and addressing their value orientation towards the public and internally towards their employees." He points out that companies often need help in communicating their corporate goals in such a way that they are not accused of immoral behavior. Companies should be able to position themselves in such a way that their business activities do not contradict their moral principles. In this respect, the Ethics Council would like to contribute to "making the mechanisms of ethics and morality in the social discourse at the interface with the economy more transparent and more conscious." The Ethics Council recommends that companies appoint ethics officers (Ethics Council 2024).

Ethics officers act on behalf of the management. They are responsible for all issues that arise in the day-to-day running of the company. Employees can turn to them if they recognize an ethical problem. Ethics officers should advise the company, but also monitor it when it comes to ethically questionable activities or areas of work. They are also responsible for conducting ethics training (Wirtschaftslexikon 2024).

Skills are required for this area of responsibility. In addition to appropriate legal knowledge, the representatives must have a good overview of all processes in the company. They should have a high level of communication skills, as conflicts of interest may arise that need to be mediated. Moral integrity is also an important quality. A commitment to leadership should be a matter of course (Schützold 2024).

Of course, ethics committees and similar organizational units can also be set up, depending on the size of the company. A connection to the Ethics Council is always an advantage.

In addition to issues relating to internal operations (e.g. dealing with employees) and the social problem areas of human rights, anti-corruption and data protection, major ethical issues also include the extensive topic of sustainability.

2.5.3 Sustainability

Sustainability is an ethical issue that extends to the smallest units of social life. Sustainability is linked to climate and environmental protection. For half of German customers, an important decision criterion for a product is whether the company behaves in a socially and economically responsible manner. There is an increasing expectation that companies will go beyond the legally prescribed behavior. A number of criteria are interlinked here. Social conduct can, for example, relate to production abroad. The consideration of responsible working conditions is then often linked to the sustainable manufacture of products. For example, companies can include in their corporate ethics that their products do not cause any social or environmental damage.

The area of ecological responsibility relates primarily to climate protection, CO_2 emissions and the consumption of resources. The economic responsibility that a company assumes is reflected in the entire value chain (jobteaser 2024).

The legal guidelines on sustainability are becoming stricter. The Supply Chain Act is currently (2024) under discussion. In addition, the EU guidelines on sustainability reporting, known as the Corporate Sustainability Reporting Directive (CSRD), are to become binding at national level. The obligation to report on sustainability will also affect many SMEs (CSRD 2024).

Companies are therefore acting in their own best interests when they pay attention to sustainability, at the risk of having to change key processes. Sustainability is of strategic importance, which is why it should be included in the general corporate strategy and thus become a task for management and executives. At the same time, an increasingly critical clientele is being served. Consumers are paying more and more attention to whether the items they spend money on meet the criteria of environmental protection and sustainability. This is also linked to health aspects, as more and more people are paying attention to their diet. Sustainability is increasingly becoming a quality feature. Decisive points include ensuring that food is not wasted and that plastic waste is avoided.

The issue of sustainability has also found its way into the investment world. More and more people who invest money want to be sure that their investments do not serve ecologically or socially irresponsible projects.

Sustainability pays off in the long run. Companies that go beyond the required legal regulations have good prospects for growth. In terms of market presence, they can strengthen their brand and enhance the value of their products. But economic gain is also possible. Raw material recycling, for example, is worthwhile. However, companies also need the courage to innovate. They need to analyze their processes and look for previously untapped potential, and they need modern technology (Deloitte 2024).

The Canadian media company Corporate Knights created the "Corporate Knights Index" in 2005. Each year, it names the 100 most sustainable companies worldwide.

2024 were on the list (corporate knights 2024):

1. Sims Ltd

This is an Australian company that specializes in the recycling of metals. It makes a significant contribution to reducing negative environmental impacts by recycling metals, thereby saving resources and reducing waste.

2. Brambles Ltd

Brambles Ltd. is an Australian company that specializes in supply chain management solutions (coordination and optimization of value and supply chains). It helps to reduce waste and improve sustainability in the logistics industry by optimizing the use and reuse of resources.

3. Vestas Wind Systems A/S

This is a Danish company that specializes in the manufacture of wind turbines. Vestas contributes to the reduction of CO_2 emissions and the promotion of clean energy.

The companies Nordex SE (manufacture, installation and maintenance of wind turbines) and SMA Solar Technology AG are ranked 5th and 10th respectively.

Companies that have included sustainability in their ethical program are generally also committed to social and labor standards, equal rights and leadership, and the use of control mechanisms.

They then comply with the rules known internationally as ESG (Environmental, Social and Corporate Governance). These cover three areas, which are summarized here under the aspect of sustainability, namely

- the impact of a company on the environment,
- a company's relationships with its stakeholders (persons, groups and institutions that are directly or indirectly involved in the company's activities) and
- the way in which a company is managed and controlled (Wikipedia 2024).

Globally, the United Nations is also committed to sustainability. Its goals in this regard include "sustained, inclusive and sustainable economic growth, full and productive employment and decent work for all". Other objectives include reducing the consumption of resources and cutting CO_2 emissions.

In an article, the University of Kassel points out that these goals can only be achieved if companies employ a diverse workforce. Only the interplay of leadership management and a corporate culture of mutual recognition can create the opportunity to establish the process of sustainability in a company. The value chain can only be successfully converted to sustainability if inclusion takes place at the same time (Uni Kassel 2024).

Literature

Kundenorientierung 2017, Kundenorientierung braucht eine neue Unternehmensorganisation, retrieved 26.01.2024, https://www.absatzwirtschaft.de/kundenorientierung-braucht-eine-neue-unternehmensorganisation-216369/

consulting-btb 2024, ORGANIZATIONAL FORMS: COMPANIES IN CHANGE, accessed 26.01.2024, NEW https://consulting-btb.de/neue-organisationsformen/

Con Cubo 2023 Successfully introducing the right organizational structure, retrieved 26.01.2024, https://www.con-cubo.com/blog/die-passende-organisationsstruktur-erfolgreich-einfuhren

Amazon 2023, *Improve the customer experience with ML-powered personalization*, retrieved 09.01.2024, https://aws.amazon.com/de/personalize/

Wikipedia 2024, *Machine learning*, retrieved 01.02.2024, https://de.wikipedia.org/wiki/Maschinelles_Lernen

Copetri 2021, *Working Backwards - a radically customer-centric strategy for innovation*, accessed 09.01.2024, https://www.copetri.com/working-backwards-als-innovationsmethode/

Glns 2024, *Restricted Stock Units - A "new" variable remuneration element for management board members and employees of stock corporations*, retrieved 03.02.2024, https://www.glns.de/aktuelles/newsletter/2020/restrictedstockunits/

Deloitte 2024, *New world of work demanding, flexible and digital*, retrieved 09.01.2024, https://www2.deloitte.com/de/de/pages/human-capital/articles/neue-arbeitswelt-studie.html

Deloitte 2023, *Human Capital Trends 2023*, accessed 09.01.2024, https://www2.deloitte.com/de/de/pages/human-capital/articles/human-capital-trends-deutschland.html

New forms of organization: Companies in transition, retrieved 26.01.2024, https://consulting-btb.de/neue-organisationsformen/

bpb 2023, *Federal Agency for Civic Education 2023, The impact of artificial intelligence on the labor market*, accessed 02.01.2024, https://www.bpb.de/themen/arbeit/arbeitsmarktpolitik/522513/die-auswirkungen-von-kuenstlicher-intelligenz-auf-den-arbeitsmarkt/

inform-software 2020, *AUTOMATIZING ROUTINE TASKS IN LOGISTICS, EVALUATING JOBS*, retrieved 10.02.2024, https://www.inform-software.com/de/blog/supply-chain-management/routineaufgaben-in-der-logistik-automatisieren-jobs-aufwerten

Federal Statistical Office 2021, *Small and medium-sized enterprises*, retrieved 08.02.2024, https://www.destatis.de/DE/Themen/Branchen-Unternehmen/Unternehmen/Kleine-Unternehmen-Mittlere-Unternehmen/_inhalt.html

Digitalzentrum-chemnitz 2024, *Rethinking business models!*, Retrieved 08.02.2024, https://digitalzentrum-chemnitz.de/wissen/disruptive-geschaeftsmodelle/

Heidenreich 2020, *The organizations of the knowledge society*, retrieved 09.02.2024, https://www.researchgate.net/publication/251815816_Die_Organisationen_der_Wis sensgesellschaft

greatplacetowork 2022, *Agility: How to establish an agile culture in your company*, accessed 09.01.2024, https://www.greatplacetowork.at/agilitaet/

Heidenberger 2023, Burkhard Heidenberger, *Corporate values 2023 - why they are important*, retrieved 13.02.2024, https://www.zeitblueten.com/news/unternehmenswerte/

rexx-systems 2024, *360 degree feedback*, retrieved 13.02.2024, https://www.rexx-systems.com/360-grad-feedback/

greatplacetowork 2022, *Agility: How to establish an agile culture in your company*, accessed 09.01.2024, https://www.greatplacetowork.at/agilitaet/

Homann 2023, *Business ethics: Why ethical corporate governance pays off*, accessed February 14, 2024, https://www.eqs.com/de/compliance-wissen/blog/unternehmensethik/#:~:text=wird%20k%C3%BCnftig%20unverzichtba r-
,Was%20versteht%20man%20unter%20Unternehmensethik%3F,mit%20moralisc hen%20Aspekten%20vereinbaren%20l%C3%A4sst.

Heidenberger 2023, Burkhard Heidenberger, *Corporate values 2023 - why they are important*, retrieved 13.02.2024, https://www.zeitblueten.com/news/unternehmenswerte/

Merkur 2024, *After BASF's withdrawal from China's Uyghur region of Xinjiang: Pressure is now growing on VW*, retrieved 15.02.2024, https://www.merkur.de/wirtschaft/menschenrechte-uiguren-china-basf-rueckzug-xinjiang-druck-vw-zr-92828255.html

zdf 2024, *BASF withdraws from Xinjiang*, retrieved 15.02.2024, https://www.zdf.de/nachrichten/politik/ausland/basf-rueckzug-xinjiang-100.html

BASF 2024, *Responsible representation of interests*, accessed February 15, 2024, https://www.basf.com/global/de/who-we-are/politics/responsible-lobbying.html

ethikverband 2024, *What we stand for*, retrieved 14.02,2024, https://www.ethikverband.de/ueber-uns

wirtschaftslexikon 2024, *Ethics Officer*, accessed February 15, 2024, https://www.wirtschaftslexikon24.com/e/ethik-beauftragte/ethik-beauftragte.htm

Schützold 2024, Philosopher Clemens Schützold: What does an ethics officer do? Retrieved 16.02.2024, https://versinnbessert.de/was-macht-ein-ethikbeauftragter/

jobteaser 2024, ETHICS & BUSINESS 2021, accessed on 13.02.2024, https://www.jobteaser.com/de/advices/ethik-im-unternehmen-das-wichtigste-zur-corporate-social-responsibility

Wikipedia 2024, Environmental, Social and Governance, retrieved 15.02.2024, https://de.wikipedia.org/wiki/Environmental,_Social_and_Governance#Bedeutung_und_Auswirkungen_von_ESG

CSRD 2024, Federal Ministry of Labor and Social Affairs 2024, Corporate Sustainability Reporting Directive (CSRD), retrieved 17.02.2024, https://www.csr-in-deutschland.de/

deloitte 2024, Responsibility as an opportunity: the transformation topic of sustainability, retrieved 17.02.2024, https://www2.deloitte.com/de/de/pages/risk/articles/sustainability-transformation.html

Corporate knights 2024, The Global 100 list: How the world's most sustainable corporations are driving the green transition, retrieved 17.02.2024, https://www.corporateknights.com/rankings/global-100-rankings/2024-global-100-rankings/the-20th-annual-global-100/

uni-kassel 2024, Die Bedeutung von Diversität und Inklusion für nachhaltige Unternehmen und Lieferketten, accessed 17.02.2024, https://www. uni-kassel .de/forschung/just/forschungsschwerpunkte/die-bedeutung-von-diversitaet-und-inklusion-fuer-nachhaltige-unternehmen-und-lieferketten

3 Focus on employees

Hyper Leadership affects all people who are at risk of exclusion due to their minority and certain attributes, but also women because they are still disadvantaged in economic processes. Diverse teams demonstrably work more effectively, to a higher quality and more innovatively. They are indispensable for entrepreneurial growth.

3.1 The facets of leadership

The term leadership has become commonplace when it comes to perceiving diverse people on an equal footing. This is a prerequisite for treating them equally.

The management consultancy Deloitte reported that in 2021 and 2022, large multinational corporations invested over 210 billion US dollars to publicly promote greater Hyper Leadership, equity and inclusion. These initiatives declared the objective of providing employees with optimized opportunities and development possibilities as well as better access to resources. In addition, historical and social restrictions should be removed (Deloitte 2023).

Such measures show that companies are committed to a corporate culture that embraces Hyper Leadership. This trend must be reinforced from an economic and social perspective in order to ensure stability and progress.

What does Hyper Leadership mean? First of all, Hyper Leadership refers to the fact that there are differences between people. The term encompasses individual, social and structural differences, but also similarities between people and groups. Some differences are evaluated in such a way that discrimination arises. This happens at all social levels and also in companies.

Various dimensions can be identified in which Hyper Leadership is recorded by individuals and which often lead to disadvantages and even discrimination. These are core areas that affect the personality, as well as external and organizational dimensions that can be found in companies (Charta der Vielfalt 2023, Erwachsenenbildung 2013).

The core areas are:
- the religion or world view
- the age or generation
- sexual orientation or sexual identity
- gender or identification with a gender
- a disability or impairment
- the ethnic origin or nationality
- the skin color
- the language, the dialect
- the appearance

External dimensions are:
- behavior during leisure time
- the habits
- the social origin
- the marital status and the question of parenthood
- the geographical location of the place of residence
- the appearance
- the professional experience
- the training
- the income

Organizational dimensions are:
- the function or classification in the company
- the field of work or the content of the work
- the department, unit, group or team
- the duration of the affiliation
- the place of work (e.g. in which branch)
- Membership of a trade union
- the management status
- Membership of networks
- seniority (principle of giving priority to people who are older or have been with the company for longer)

Employees identify similarities or differences in all areas. Factors that have nothing to do with work play a significant role in the assessments of colleagues. A company that promotes and cultivates Hyper Leadership must always be aware of this and counteract prejudices.

Every factor that falls under Hyper Leadership can serve the company well. The chances of achieving good results thanks to Hyper Leadership even increase if several diverse employees work together within a team. We then speak of hyper-diverse teams. Although it is currently most important to establish leadership to a greater extent in companies, these teams are the future, albeit a somewhat distant one. They represent a paradigm shift in the way companies approach inclusion and talent management. In a world that is becoming increasingly globalized, hyper-diverse teams are becoming the driving force for innovation and success. They are a dynamic amalgamation of diverse individuals who bring unique perspectives, experiences and skills to the table. As such, they are challenging conventional notions of homogeneity in the workplace. They embrace leadership in the broadest sense.

Examples of the effectiveness of hyper-diverse teams are:

In demographic terms

The interaction of employees of different ages, different physical abilities, different ethnicities and nationalities and different sexual orientations.

In cultural terms

The interaction of employees with different cultural or religious backgrounds and with different languages or dialects (in many countries there are several, sometimes very different dialects, for example in China and India).

With regard to professional experience

The interaction of employees with different professional qualifications and careers and from different sectors.

With regard to educational history

The interaction of employees with different qualifications, further training and certifications, but also with skills that they bring with them outside of their professional background.

With regard to the individual working method and personal disposition

The interaction between extroverted and introverted people, as well as between people who are more creative and those who are more analytical, and also between people who work systematically but follow different systems (e.g. more empirical or more deductive).

With regard to global representation

The interaction of employees from different regions, countries, continents and time zones.

Assembling teams that are diverse in as many respects as possible has several advantages. This approach is in line with the company's social responsibility, increases efficiency in most cases after a short time and generates a greater reputation in the public eye and therefore among customers.

Diverse teams often make optimal decisions. This can be explained by the fact that the different perspectives lead to a more thorough analysis than in homogeneous groups, resulting in a more accurate outcome. In addition, diverse teams are more adaptable to change than groups with a comparable mentality and mindset. They cover a broad spectrum of skills and perspectives, which enables them to react more quickly and efficiently to changes that arise in the business environment. This adaptability is a key criterion for surviving in global markets. Diverse groups are better able to identify and understand the needs and preferences of a wide range of customers. This is the prerequisite for developing appropriate offers and expanding the customer base.

Diverse people themselves naturally feel most comfortable in companies where they can develop their full potential without discrimination. Inclusion gives companies the opportunity to achieve top performance through the interaction of the many different ways in which the human species develops.

The link between leadership and business success is confirmed by the results of an international analysis conducted by the McKinsey research institute (McKinsey 2020). It found that the more diverse a company is, the greater its success. The study "Diversity Wins - How Inclusion Matters" collected data from over 1,000 companies in 15 countries.

In the study, McKinsey examined diversity with regard to gender, ethnicity and nationality. The inclusion of these three criteria has already led to considerable operational results. Companies increase the probability of above-average profitability by 25% if they have a high level of gender diversity. In the comparative study from 2014, the probability was still at 15%, which shows the increasing importance of gender management. If the board of directors of a company is ethnically and nationally diverse, the probability can even increase by 36%.

According to the study, many companies neglected the fact that leadership in particular should be diverse. It showed that only 33% of companies had improved in this respect over the previous five years, but again only 5% had improved significantly. Accordingly, one result was that the companies with the lowest consideration of diversity in terms of gender and ethnicity/nationality were the least likely to be more profitable than average.

McKinsey also examined the assessments of 30,000 employees on the topics of diversity and inclusive corporate culture. The result was that just over half of employees perceived diversity as existing in the company and 31% did not. The survey also analyzed how employees experience equal opportunities, openness and a sense of belonging in their company. 29 % saw such an inclusive corporate culture as existing, but 61 % saw it as non-existent.

As a bottom line, the research company pointed out that the use of all kinds of "quota people" is useless. Formal solutions do not work. Managers must stand behind diversity and exemplify it.

Defining Hyper Leadership and Hyper Agility in the Modern Workforce

In an era marked by unprecedented change, traditional leadership models and organizational structures are proving insufficient to meet contemporary challenges. Two interconnected concepts have emerged as critical elements for organizational success: hyper leadership and hyper agility. This chapter establishes comprehensive definitions for these terms and explores their significance in today's workforce.

Hyper Leadership Core Definition

Hyper Leadership is an elevated form of leadership that transcends traditional hierarchical models by embracing diversity, fostering inclusive practices, and leveraging collective intelligence across all dimensions of organizational life. It represents a dynamic, multi-dimensional approach to leading organizations through complex, rapidly changing environments.

Key Characteristics

1. Inclusive Decision-Making
- Integration of diverse perspectives
- Collaborative problem-solving
- Distributed authority
- Collective wisdom utilization

2. Adaptive Mindset
- Continuous learning orientation
- Comfort with ambiguity
- Rapid response capability
- Innovation focus

3. Cultural Intelligence
- Cross-cultural competence
- Global perspective
- Demographic awareness
- Social sensitivity

4. Transformational Influence
- Inspirational motivation
- Individual consideration
- Intellectual stimulation
- Ethical behavior modeling

Hyper Agility Core Definition

Hyper agility refers to an organization's enhanced capability to rapidly adapt, transform, and innovate in response to changing conditions while maintaining operational effectiveness. It represents a state of organizational fluidity that enables swift, purposeful change across multiple dimensions simultaneously.

Key Dimensions

1. Structural Agility
- Flexible organizational design
- Rapid reconfiguration capability
- Network-based operations
- Dynamic team formation

2. Process Agility
- Adaptive workflows
- Streamlined procedures
- Quick decision pathways
- Iterative improvement cycles

3. Cultural Agility
- Change readiness
- Innovation mindset
- Learning orientation
- Resilience capacity

4. Workforce Agility
- Skill adaptability
- Role flexibility
- Cross-functional capabilities
- Continuous learning

The Interconnection: Symbiotic Relationship

Hyper Leadership and hyper agility exist in a mutually reinforcing relationship where:

1. Leadership Enables Agility
- Creates supportive environment
- Removes barriers
- Provides resources
- Encourages experimentation

2. Agility Enhances Leadership
- Provides feedback loops
- Enables rapid adjustment
- Supports innovation
- Facilitates learning

Contextual Factors - Environmental Drivers

1. Technological Advancement
- Digital transformation
- Automation impact
- Communication evolution
- Virtual collaboration

2. Demographic Shifts
- Generational diversity
- Cultural integration
- Changing workforce expectations
- Global talent mobility

3. Market Dynamics
- Global competition
- Industry convergence
- Customer expectations
- Innovation speed

Organizational Impact - Transformation Areas

1. Structure
- Flatter hierarchies
- Network organizations
- Matrix relationships
- Dynamic teams

2. Systems
- Flexible processes
- Adaptive technologies
- Integrated communications
- Learning platforms

3. Culture
- Innovation mindset
- Inclusive practices
- Collaborative norms
- Change readiness

Measurement Framework - Key Indicators

1. Leadership Effectiveness
- Decision quality
- Team engagement
- Innovation rate
- Change success

2. Organizational Agility
- Response time
- Adaptation speed
- Innovation implementation
- Performance stability

Future Evolution - Emerging Trends

1. Technology Integration
- AI-enhanced leadership
- Virtual team dynamics
- Digital transformation
- Automated processes

2. Workforce Evolution
- Remote work integration
- Skill hybridization
- Career flexibility
- Learning acceleration

Understanding Hyper Leadership and hyper agility as distinct yet interconnected concepts is crucial for modern organizations. These definitions provide a foundation for developing practical implementation strategies and measuring success in creating more adaptive, inclusive, and effective organizations.

The evolution of these concepts will continue as organizations face new challenges and opportunities. Success in the future workplace will depend on the ability to embrace and implement both Hyper Leadership and hyper agility while maintaining alignment with organizational goals and values.

3.2 Why diverse teams are an advantage

3.2.1 Opening up broader markets

Diverse teams are the key to success in the modern world because they open up the possibility of hiring the best talent. Inclusion takes place at all levels. Of course, the more dimensions of diversity are covered, the more this applies. Hyper-diverse teams increase all opportunities.

For research and development, as for all areas of marketing, groups contain valuable skills when they are diverse. For example, in the cultural field, they have background information, skills and insights that enable the company to respond to even the nuances of different consumer preferences. They can also adapt to new or high expectations and respond to them quickly and effectively. Different cultural competencies, for example, can have a major impact on the products and services that are demanded. Subtleties often play a major role.

Even a single society is made up of different groupings. In some cases, these groups are very different from one another. Older and younger people often have communication difficulties, for example. Similarly, people of different ethnicities often come from different worlds, which can differ significantly in their attitudes, from views on educational methods and behavior in public spaces to judgments about physical appearance. A certain degree of understanding and acceptance is necessary to enable people to live together on a social level. However, the people who understand others best are those who belong to the same ethnic group or come from the same culture. This also applies to companies. This clearly shows once again that striving for diversity in the company always supports a social process of inclusion, and vice versa. The diversity of people is fundamentally natural, so it is important to deal with it appropriately, both socially and economically.

The better the needs of groups are understood, the better they can be addressed. It is not just a question of whether products/services are not yet on the market or whether existing offers should be better tailored to specific needs. Dispositions that homogeneous groups would not even think about must also be taken into account. For example, different ethnic groups categorize individual offers differently when it comes to consumer goods and luxury items. There are also differences in the need for sufficient differentiation (e.g. in terms of color nuances) or ease of use. In addition, individual regional areas may have special needs that are not yet satisfied by the market. Regional areas can be very large in some countries, such as China and India.

Different languages are a particular barrier to understanding other people. Native speakers naturally have the best opportunities to communicate with their peers. Diverse teams are able to break down language barriers. They offer the best chance of someone speaking the native language. In some cases, related languages are well understood. In large countries, however, there are also regional dialects with significant differences. In China alone, for example, there are around 100 dialects, 10 of which are considered the most important (Sprachcaffe 2022).

Successfully addressing target groups requires a comprehensive understanding on several levels. It must be ensured that campaigns and marketing activities address the target persons in such a way that they can find themselves on as many levels as possible. This makes it possible to expand the customer base and develop markets.

Jenny Gruner, Director of Global Digital Marketing at Hapag-Lloyd, is a supporter of diversity in companies. She refers to a global survey of advertisers conducted by Shutterstock. The American company is active in the areas of stock photography (producing stock images), footage (film material) and production music (Gruner 2023).

Overall, 60% of respondents considered ethnic diversity to be an important factor in successfully addressing target groups. 75% assumed that diverse content would only be considered authentic by target group members if it was (co-)created by diverse people. For Germany, it was found that 41% of advertisers find it difficult to portray brands in connection with LGBTQ content.

The American business magazine Forbes referred to a Harvard Business Review from 2013, which highlighted the importance of the affiliation factor. One finding was that the likelihood of understanding customers increases significantly in a diverse team. This is because if just one team member shares the ethnicity of a customer, it is already twice as high as in teams where no one shares the ethnicity. This example alone can be used to calculate how much market opportunities increase in connection with diversity (Forbes 2020).

Markets that have not yet been tapped into or that were previously considered untapped can only be conquered if diversity is integrated. This insight has become established with varying degrees of clarity in different countries. This is shown by further results of the Shutterstock study (Shutterstock 2021). The following results were found in the area of marketing:

Attitude surveyed: Agreement that equality between the male and female gender is an important factor in marketing campaigns.
1. Brazil 74 %
2. Australia 72 %
3. Italy 70 %
4. France 69 %
5. South Korea 68 %
6. Spain 66 %
7. USA 65 %
8. United Kingdom 63 %
9. Germany 53 %

Fact under investigation: Inclusion of depictions of homosexual couples and non-traditional families in marketing campaigns.
1. Australia 25 %
2. Spain 24 %
3. USA 23 %
4. Italy 22 %
5. Brazil 21 %

6. France 19 %
7. United Kingdom 16 %
8. Germany 12 %
9. South Korea 5 %

Investigated fact: Inclusion of the "Black Lives Matter" and "Stop Asian Hate movements" in marketing campaigns.
1. Australia 73 %
2. Brazil 71 %
3. France 69 %
4. Spain 63 %
5. USA 61 %
6. United Kingdom 61 %
7. Italy 58 %
8. Germany 54 %
9. South Korea 52 %

Attitude surveyed: Agreement that more people with disabilities need to be portrayed in visual media.
1. Brazil 73 %
2. Australia 71 %
3. Italy 69 %
4. USA 63 %
5. United Kingdom 61 %
6. France 61 %
7. Spain 58 %
8. South Korea 54 %
9. Germany 52 %

Investigated fact: Increased representation of people over 50 in marketing campaigns in the last 12 months.
1. Australia 31 %
2. Brazil 22 %
3. France 20 %

4. Spain 18 %
5. USA 17 %
6. United Kingdom 17 %
7. Italy 17 %
8. Germany 12 %
9. South Korea 11 %

Marketing campaigns are not isolated measures. They reflect the attitude of companies. As the results show, it is becoming increasingly important and urgent to establish diverse teams for these important projects as well.

3.2.2 Higher quality

Every company depends on delivering the right quality for its target groups. In this respect, the quality of products and services is a strong cornerstone for success.

Diversity secures this cornerstone. Diverse teams bring a wealth of expertise and specialist know-how to the table. They guarantee that the status quo is not simply accepted. Tasks are viewed from a wide variety of perspectives, which automatically increases the quality of the result. The more intensive and detailed the analyses are, the higher the quality of the findings and their implementation. At the same time, a culture of innovation is created and driven forward.

Diversity marketing brings a company decisively forward. It takes into account the diversity of consumers, the entire customer base and the workforce. Tapping into the full potential of employees ensures quality that can hold its own in the markets. A 2019 study by the American market analysis company Marketing Charts found that 34% of customers ignore a brand whose marketing does not represent them (Gruner 2023).

If a company does without employees who represent a certain group of diverse people, it can quickly lose out on profits. One target group that is still neglected by the public is people with disabilities. If they and their interests were more strongly reflected in diversity marketing, further markets could be opened up. There are individual approaches. For example, ZDF wants to focus on accessible television advertising together with a major consumer goods provider (2024).

These are measures that lead to a qualitative improvement. How good it would be if companies had a sufficient number of people with disabilities in their ranks. They would strengthen the quality of diversity marketing. Of course, this applies to all areas of diversity. It is crucial for the quality of a company to reach the breadth of society and not just the average. The average excludes entire groups.

Of course, disputes are also to be expected in various groups. It is important to establish a good communication culture here. Appropriate training supports an appropriate and respectful discussion, which often has to be learned first. It is often neglected in school and social processes. But the effort pays off. Hyper Leadership leads to a kind of reflection and rethinking that more homogeneous groups do not achieve. Here it is much more likely that equality of thought will prevail. You don't leave the level of agreement either, because the points of view are the same and nobody sees the need or would feel good about bringing completely different aspects into play. In diverse teams, every member is prepared for unexpected alternatives to be mentioned that no one can ignore. Extensive discussions and the weighing up of many arguments are to be expected in order to find a consensus. One's own points of view must be expanded, which leads to a better understanding of other views. In addition, thinking in diverse teams is not linear, as is often the case in homogeneous groups. This results in a more intensive and qualitatively better way of working, which leads to optimal results.

When working together in diverse teams, it doesn't just have to be about the classic categorization of diversity. Hyperdiversity is often easy to incorporate. Examples include employees with different industry backgrounds, experience abroad or from a completely different field of study. Career changes often bring in additional points of view. All of these factors can significantly increase quality and drive growth in the market.

Diverse groups are more productive. In 2020, the American business magazine Forbes reported on an American study that examined listed US companies with regard to diversity. It confirmed that socially diverse groups are both more innovative and more productive. This is consistent with findings from economic and demographic studies (Forbes 2020).

3.2.3 Growth

The more diverse a company's teams are, the greater the chance of generating growth, including exponential growth. Different backgrounds and diverse horizons of experience not only generate creative energy, but also synergy effects.

Successes can already be seen when a company takes a few or even just one factor into account, deviating from the conventional pattern of its HR policy. One example was reported by the American business magazine Forbes 2020 based on a study by the Credit Suisse Research Institute (Forbes 2020). It found that companies with one or more women on the board achieved better economic growth than companies with only male board members. A greater return on investment (ROI) was found. As this is a key figure that provides information on whether an investment has paid off, it is an objectively measurable value. Gender diversity alone therefore pays off. Despite this, 77% of the boards of the 500 largest listed US companies were still made up of men in 2020. Only 2% were made up of 50% or more women.

Forbes also reported that the US market research company Bloomberg provided information on companies with a balanced gender ratio in their teams. According to this, they had a higher return on equity than those without this constellation.

This is not surprising given that women make the majority of all purchases. For this reason alone, they are in a position to understand processes on the market and recognize opportunities for marketing. Innovations therefore affect masses of people who bear a distinctive characteristic - female. From the point of view of offering products and services for the majority, women should be included in business processes when companies offer these things.

The fact that Hyper Leadership makes business sense was already established in 2015 with the two factors of gender diversity and ethnic diversity. This was shown in a study by the US management consultancy McKinsey (Hunt 2015). According to this study, companies that had the right staff were more likely to achieve a return on investment that was above the national industry average than companies that did not take diversity into account. In figures: Companies with ethnic diversity as well as diversity in terms of different skin colors were 35% likely and companies with diversity in terms of gender were 15% likely.

The 2018 Harvard Business Review discusses the impact of diversity in the venture capital industry (Gompers 2018). Paul Gompers, Professor of Business Administration at Harvard Business School, spent several years studying thousands of venture capitalists and tens of thousands of investments. Research had already shown that diversity in teams has a positive effect on analytical thinking, objectivity and the ability to innovate. In addition, he wanted to research the relationship between diversity and financial results. He therefore chose the venture capital industry. He assumed that every person who invests also contributes to developments and has an impact on business processes. He also considered it easy to understand which people sit on supervisory boards and what qualifications they have. He used the fact that factors such as education, gender and ethnicity can be easily analyzed in connection with financial success in this industry.

The starting point was to define the objectives of venture capital companies. Both the investors and the venture capital company itself have the goal of selecting and promoting those companies that achieve the best possible results.

Paul Gompers' research results showed that diversity significantly improves financial performance, e.g. profitable investments increased. He came to the conclusion that homogeneous groups significantly reduce such successes.

The data showed that people in the venture capital sector have worked in homogeneous groups relatively consistently since 1990. Only 8% were female and only 1% were non-white. The analyses showed that belonging to the same skin color increased the willingness to work together by 39.2 % and an educational degree from the same educational institution even by 34.4 %. This increased the likelihood of maintaining homogeneity at all levels of cooperation.

However, Gompers found that it is precisely uniformity that reduces the chances of success. His findings showed that the more similar groups working together are, the weaker their results are. For example, the success rate for acquisitions and IPOs was on average 11.5% lower when partners attended the same school than when they attended different schools. When the same ethnicity was present, the success rate fell by more than a quarter to 32.2%.

One surprising finding concerned the gender issue. Venture capital companies like to look at the number of children in the families of their partner companies. If there are more daughters than sons, the willingness to hire a woman increases by 25 %. Interestingly, the probability of hiring a female company member would increase by a quarter if a daughter were born instead of a son. In fact, the data showed that venture capital firms improved their results after increasing the proportion of women by 10%.

Gompers also reported that the positive economic impact of diversity is not limited to the venture capital sector. For example, the US National Bureau of Economic Research found in a study that there is a positive influence on the creation of products and services in the USA in the fields of law, medicine, natural sciences and management. This study examined trends in gross domestic product over 50 years starting in the 1960s. During these decades, diversity in companies increased. In particular, the employment of women and people of color increased. At the same time, the US economy grew. Assuming that innate skills are evenly distributed across genders and ethnicities, the increase in women and black people of both genders played a role in the improved economic performance of companies. The USA would therefore have a good chance of achieving further economic success if it continued to increase diversity in companies.

Gompers points out that diversity is particularly important in companies in which a small group has far-reaching and forward-looking decision-making powers. If decision-makers are diverse, Hyper Leadership is much more likely to propagate further up the hierarchy. Members of groups that are traditionally underrepresented are more likely to advocate for members of other underrepresented groups, while white men, for example, are more likely to hire white men.

Gompers also cites a survey of venture capitalists. This was about the generation of deal flows (investment proposals offered to venture capital managers). The survey revealed that the educational background, gender and skin color were largely comparable. However, such homogeneous groups hardly have different networks. However, diverse networks increase the possibilities of generating deal flows. It is therefore very likely that conventional companies are leaving some money lying around here.

Literature:

Deloitte 2023, retrieved 09.01.2024, https://www2.deloitte.com/de/de/pages/human-capital/articles/human-capital-trends-deutschland.html

Charta der Vielfalt 2023, More than "something with diversity" - What task diversity has, retrieved 21.02.2024, https://www.charta-der-vielfalt.de/

Adult Education 2013, Dimensions of Diversity, retrieved 21.02.2024, https://erwachsenenbildung.at/themen/diversitymanagement/grundlagen/dimensionen.php

McKinsey 2020, Connection between diversity and business success clearer than ever, retrieved 02.01.2023, https://www.mckinsey.com/de/news/presse/2020-05-19-diversity-wins

Gruner 2023, Jenny Gruner: Why companies benefit from diversity marketing, retrieved 28.02.2024, https://dup-magazin.de/management/marketing-vertrieb/warum-unternehmen-von-diversity-marketing-profitieren/

Shutterstock 2021, Diversity Report, accessed 28.02.2024, https://d3kqgz5iyf5gxy.cloudfront.net/CRTV+2021/Diversity+report/Diversity+Report_Updated_Forward_Final_05.pdf

Forbes 2020, Stuart R. Levine: Diversity Confirmed To Boost Innovation And Financial Results, retrieved 27.02.2024, https://www.forbes.com/sites/forbesinsights/2020/01/15/diversity-confirmed-to-boost-innovation-and-financial-results/?sh=13f11d58c4a6

Sprachcaffe 2022, The 10 most important dialects of the Chinese language, retrieved 17.03.2024, https://www.sprachcaffe.de/magazin-artikel/die-10-groessten-dialekte-der-chinesischen-sprache.htm

Gruner 2023, Jenny Gruner: Why companies benefit from diversity marketing, retrieved 03.02.2024, https://dup-magazin.de/management/marketing-vertrieb/warum-unternehmen-von-diversity-marketing-profitieren/

Forbes 2020, Stuart R. Levine: Diversity Confirmed To Boost Innovation And Financial Results, retrieved 27.02.2024, https://www.forbes.com/sites/forbesinsights/2020/01/15/diversity-confirmed-to-boost-innovation-and-financial-results/?sh=13f11d58c4a6

Forbes 2020, Diversity Confirmed To Boost Innovation And Financial Results Stuart R. Levine, retrieved 27.02.2024, https://www.forbes.com/sites/forbesinsights/2020/01/15/diversity-confirmed-to-boost-innovation-and-financial-results/?sh=13f11d58c4a6

Hunt 2015, Why diversity matters By Dame Vivian Hunt, Dennis Layton, and Sara Prince; accessed 04.03.2024, https://www.mckinsey.com/capabilities/people-and-organizational-performance/our-insights/why-diversity-matters

Gompers 2018, The Other Diversity Dividend by Paul Gompers and Silpa Kovvali, accessed 04.03.2024, https://hbr.org/2018/07/the-other-diversity-dividend

4 Attracting talent

Innovative recruitment strategies are needed to attract diverse talent. These include job boards and networks. Reflective linguistic formulations that incorporate Hyper Leadership is important. Prejudices must be avoided from the application to the selection process. Only a person's skills and development opportunities should be assessed.

4.1 Recruitment strategies for attracting talent

4.1.1 Targeted ads

One method still used to recruit staff is advertising in print editions. Both regional and national options are possible. If you choose a daily newspaper, you should not just go for the most widely circulated ones. Those who have fewer opportunities to travel long distances or change their home at short notice are dependent on regional proximity. This also applies to many diverse talents. This is why you should also use the daily newspapers in the regions. It is also important to state the exact location of the job in online advertisements.

Of course, when it comes to advertisements, it is natural to think of magazines that appeal to a specific group of people. Of course there are magazines that deal with autism or intercultural topics, for example. However, it should be noted that the readership is a select group within the diversity pool. In other words, a pre-selection is made that ignores other, equally diverse people from the outset. However, there may be situations in which a company would like to supplement its diversity, for example in the area of intercultural cooperation, or make use of the special skills of people with autism. It is therefore worth considering taking a look at the magazine landscape.

A prerequisite for the targeted selection of diverse talent is an analysis by HR of which leadership factors are covered in the company and which still need to be developed. If there is a gap here, there is nothing wrong with selecting the groups to be addressed by advertising in specialist magazines

The second option for placing advertisements is job boards. Most of them can be found online. But there are also those that are organized regionally on site. Again, it should be borne in mind that various people are often looking for a job in the region. Examples include people who, for reasons of social background, are strongly tied to their environment, are less mobile in terms of transportation or are (severely) disabled. It is therefore worth participating in such fairs with a company stand. It is particularly convincing if a relevant member of the workforce is present and can give an authentic account.

In any form of targeted recruitment, wording is very important, as are visual representations. This is where the company can show how serious it is about leadership. Many advertisements are limited to the addition of m/f/d to the personnel being sought. In the following, the generic masculine is often even used. This should be avoided. In addition, the company's own description often lacks references or signs that diverse talents can be found among the workforce. However, this should be recognizable.

One group that is often explicitly addressed in advertisements is severely disabled people and those whose disability has been equated with a severe disability. You can apply for equal status if you have a degree of disability of less than 50 percent. If approved, this is increased to 50 percent. In contrast to a severe disability of 50 percent or more, this equalization relates exclusively to employment law conditions (and not to tax benefits and the right to accompanying persons).

Addressing people with severe disabilities is required by law. The law legally stipulates integration into the world of work, which is why companies must take severely disabled people into account when filling vacancies (BIH 2022). In job advertisements, you will then read the addition: "Severely disabled people will be given preference if they have the same qualifications." Unfortunately, many companies prefer to pay the equalization levy, which is also required by law, rather than hire disabled people. There is no obligation to specifically address this group in an advertisement.

Of course, it is not possible to explain the other various attributes in the same way as the disability factor. However, it is possible to address as many people with different backgrounds as possible on a linguistic and visual level.

Let's take an example from the field of gender. Statistics show that male applicants apply for a job if they have around 60 percent of the skills and knowledge required (surveymonkey 2023). As a rule, such skills are listed in job advertisements as a prerequisite for applying or filling a position. Women, on the other hand, only write their application if they assume that they fulfill 100 percent of the requirements.

In order to adequately include female applicants, it is possible to refrain from mentioning a specific number of years of professional experience in the advertisement. In this case, this would also suit many women who have not worked for child-rearing reasons. One shouldn't ask for "x years of professional experience", for example, but limit yourself to general statements such as "professional experience is necessary" or even just "professional experience is desirable".

This necessitates a sensitive questioning of the usual wording in job advertisements. In the above example, one can further consider whether professional experience is actually indispensable. Perhaps this profession does not even exist in other cultures. But perhaps there are related professions. A transitional phase may then be possible in which the skills can be completed. It is therefore important to reconsider whether entrenched standards are appropriate in advertisements.

If we now assume that, for example, people with a different ethnic background also question themselves critically, then a woman with an ethnic background other than the usual national background already has two factors that could trigger discrimination. The same applies, for example, to a person with a cultural background that is different from the usual national background and who also has a sexual orientation that is different from the binary sexual orientation. If one considers that other manifestations of leadership such as age or ethnicity can be added, further double, if not triple, inhibiting factors quickly emerge.

Phrases such as "We are a young, dynamic team of engineers" may be an accurate way to present yourself, but it puts off or excludes several people from being motivated to apply - in this case, especially older and female people, regardless of their background.

Some expressions offer alternatives on a more subtle level. For example, the term "a craftsman's business" can be replaced by "a craftswomen's business". This breaks with the usual forms of expression and encourages diverse talents.

Formulating texts in advertisements in a leadership-friendly way is a deliberate, conscious process. It is important not to be too specific so that a broad group is addressed. On the other hand, a company naturally wants to fill a position with a suitable candidate. It is therefore advisable to focus on the skills and knowledge that are required. Key qualifications such as reliability or the ability to work in a team are also not associated with the risk of making an exclusionary pre-selection.

It should be avoided to require a specific degree, for example from an elite university or a private university (surveymonkey 2023). It is better to require a specialist degree and to name it as such in general terms. This provides a wide scope. Anyone who does not have a university career but has a comparable qualification can also find themselves here.

Both advertisements and job boards should include visual incentives for Lladership. There are fewer options for advertisements, but even here the company can post at least one image that signals leadership in the selection of personnel. Be it a person in a wheelchair, a non-white person or a team in which diverse talents are visible.

Images are highly expressive. Most people react strongly to visual stimuli. You should therefore choose carefully which images you use for job fairs, especially those that take place on site. The images should be as authentic as they are credible. At first glance, a specific job, suitably staffed, already says a lot. A diverse team in a meeting has the same effect. There is no need to exaggerate and avoid non-diverse people. The overall picture is convincing.

The company can also be presented with the help of facts and figures. For example, you can show the proportion of older or female employees or those who come from a different cultural background. If you want to increase the numbers, you can easily show this in a graphical representation. In this way, diverse talents feel addressed from the outset when looking for work. The decisive factor here is that they are given an indication of their identification with the company.

Other options are to provide information that is particularly relevant for various employees. For example, you could show all the countries from which employees come on a map (surveymonkey 2023) and provide them with additional information, e.g. number of inhabitants, predominant religions, form of government, etc. It is also a good idea to present an appealing text in the native language of each country, going beyond a simple "Welcome".

If you want to make sure you express yourself in a leadership-friendly way, you can use guidelines. Guidelines can be found online or in book form. However, it is also advisable to draw up a corresponding checklist for your own company.

Literature

autistenhilfe 2023, SPECIAL FEATURES IN COMMUNICATION, retrieved 16.08.2023, https://www.autistenhilfe.at/was-ist-autismus/hauptmerkmale/besonderheiten-der-autismus-spektrum-stoerung-ass/

BIH 2022, Employment obligation, accessed 16.08.2023, https://www.bih.de/integrationsaemter/medien-und-publikationen/fachlexikon/detail/beschaeftigungspflicht/#:~:text=Jeder%20Arbeitgebe r%20mit%20jahresdurchschnittlich%20mindestens,(%C2%A7%20154%20SGB %20IX)

Surveymonkey 2023, Diversity and inclusion in recruitment, accessed 14.08.2023, https://www.surveymonkey.de/mp/Diversity-recruiting/

4.1.2 Networks

New employees are often recruited exclusively from external sources. However, HR management can easily overlook the opportunities that the existing workforce has to offer. Here you can learn from the approach taken by the public sector. If you are looking to fill a vacancy in an office, a public authority, an association or a professional association, the position is usually advertised internally first. There are many positions in the civil service without civil servants; in 2023, only 37% of positions were filled by civil servants (studieren.de 2023). In addition, there are employment relationships equivalent to the civil service, namely public corporations, institutions and foundations (Rechtswörterbuch 2023).

Internal job advertisements create opportunities for employees to change jobs. Without such advertisements, they might not even have heard about the vacancy. Only if the position cannot be filled internally is it advertised externally.

The private sector is obliged to advertise internally as soon as the company has a works council. Sections 75 and 93 of the Works Constitution Act stipulate that the works council can request an internal advertisement for vacant positions, with the exception of senior executives (Federal Ministry of Justice 2023).

An internal job advertisement must include all factors that also apply to an external search, from the requirements to the contact person in the HR office. This is where diversity recruiting for diverse talent can come in.

It is possible to adopt the practice of internal job advertisements in principle. It is important to use wording in such a way that diverse people and also women feel addressed (if women are underrepresented). This differentiation is important because women represent around 50% of people, while it is typical for diverse people to belong to the statistical minority. Many women feel addressed with words such as "team-oriented, committed, reliable, dedicated, cooperative", many men with terms such as "challenging, individual, logical, above-average, direct" (hr-rocket 2023). So there is a difference between offering a job that requires "team spirit, reliability and a willingness to cooperate" and one that demands "above-average commitment, logical thinking and direct communication". Of course, it is important to remain objective. Of course there are jobs that require special key qualifications such as the ability to work in a team or skills such as logical thinking. But these skills are not tied to one gender or to the characteristics of different people.

An internal job advertisement should take leadership into account. Diverse people who see themselves better suited to a different job have the same opportunity for change as everyone else in the workforce. However, it may be that they are more likely to have the confidence to move within a company where they already work. If they do, this sense of achievement strengthens their loyalty to the company.

The idea of internal job advertisements offers another possibility. If the legal requirement is not met, the position can still be advertised internally and employees can be informed that a vacancy is being sought and that various people are welcome. Employees are asked to encourage suitable people in their personal circle or networks to apply. The strategy of such employee referrals is still underestimated. Many families contain people with disabilities, for example, and there are various talented individuals in the circle of many families. These sources are multiplied if you include the networks of family members. This opens up recruiting options that tend to expand. You also need to bear in mind that the various employees you already employ often have their own specific community that they can inform.

Networks are generally an excellent resource for HR management that focuses on leadership. There are 2 options. Employees can be encouraged to build their own networks, or existing external networks can be used. Commerzbank offers an example of how to encourage employees to establish their own networks.

The Bank used the "Diversity Charter" back in 2007. This is one of the largest initiatives by employers to promote diversity in companies and institutions in Germany (Charta der Vielfalt 2023). The association was launched in 2006 as a joint initiative by companies and political initiatives and serves to recognize and incorporate diversity into working life. Anyone who joins receives a certificate with the title "Diversity Charter" for an administrative fee. It is worthwhile for employers to purchase it and display it prominently in the entrance area.

Commerzbank should serve here as an example of the paths that can be taken internally. It encouraged its employees to set up their own company networks. The topics for this were diverse and came from the employees themselves. The various individuals were thus able to focus on their specific concerns, interests and knowledge. This resulted in a whole series of initiatives. The start-ups covered a wide variety of areas. One network focused on people with non-binary sexual orientation, another on the interaction between people of different ethnicities or cultural interests. One network was aimed specifically at women, while another focused on the topic of "care". One father set up a network specifically for people in the same family role. Employees with a Christian faith set up a network for Christians. One foundation invited people with and without disabilities to come together (Personalwirtschaft 2021).

This gives employees a safe space in which they can exchange ideas. There is a representation medium for the respective group and its concerns. The company management has the opportunity to obtain information at any time. This improves communication between the hierarchical levels. A working atmosphere characterized by mutual understanding is promoted.

Such networks are a treasure trove for new diverse employees. Of course, they also serve non-diverse people. However, encouraging the creation of networks within the company is fundamentally an integrative or inclusive human resources management measure. This not only increases contacts between employees, but also intensifies their identification with the company. It also strengthens a working atmosphere in which diverse talents work together as a matter of course.

Even if these are internal company networks, each member has numerous external contacts. These relationships can be put to good use when recruiting diverse personnel. Employees only need to know about the job advertisement.

A company can also use external networks itself. Again, it makes sense to first ask employees which ones they know. At the same time, they can be encouraged to inform their contacts about a vacancy themselves.

Of course, searching in external networks requires the corresponding time capacity in HR management. However, it is possible to concentrate on the initiatives with a focus on diversity that you would like to supplement. One way to obtain information, for example, is the "A World of Diversity" network. The association has built up a broad platform for the areas of diversity and anti-discrimination. It is a member of many relevant associations and has an international network in some cases. Contact details can be found here. There is also an extensive list of further publications and links on the topics of diversity and anti-discrimination (Eine Welt der Vielfalt 2023).

In principle, it is advantageous to network at many levels of society. This also includes offices such as the Federal Anti-Discrimination Agency (Antidiskriminierungsstelle des Bundes 2023). One example of this is the company ISS. It works closely with customers and authorities. Its aim is to create career opportunities for people who often have limited opportunities to find and develop work. ISS operates worldwide, including in Germany and the Netherlands. The company works with regional labor markets, local and national authorities and numerous organizations that support diversity (issworld 2023).

Young diverse people often have problems finding a job. Some are disadvantaged in terms of cultural requirements, language skills and little experience in dealing with their Hyper Leadership within social contexts due to their age. One way to get in touch with them is through university networks. One initiative that operates nationwide at this level is the Diversity Network (Netzwerk-Diversity 2023). Members are not the universities themselves, but natural persons. Contact persons are available on the website.

Many young people with physical or mental disabilities, as well as learning disabilities, still belong to socially disadvantaged groups. They often cannot find a training position in the private sector. For this reason, there are vocational training centers that provide inter-company training. During this time, they try to establish contacts with companies that temporarily train the trainees on site. However, this is not always successful. For people with disabilities, it is particularly important that they find a job after their training. Their chances decrease as they get older. Unemployed people without disabilities are more than twice as likely to find a job as unemployed people with disabilities. Nowadays, there are many technical aids that compensate for disabilities. Digitalization in particular offers many opportunities. (aktion mensch 2022)

The national contact point for people with disabilities who are being trained in vocational training centers is the Federal Association of Vocational Training Centers (bagbbw 2023). For recruitment purposes, it is worth getting in touch with a nearby vocational training center. There are more than 50 of these facilities in Germany, spread across the federal states. Incidentally, the Federal Employment Agency generally grants integration assistance when taking on a person with a disability in order to strengthen their inclusion.

Literature

Studieren.de 2023, I want to become a civil servant, retrieved 22.08.2023, https://studieren.de/beamter-werden.0.html

Legal Dictionary 2023, Public Service, retrieved 22.08.2023, https://www.rechtswoerterbuch.de/recht/o/oeffentlicher-dienst/#:~:text=Der%20%C3%B6ffentliche%20Dienst%20umfasst%20alle,K%C3%B6rperschaft%2C%20Anstalt%20oder%20Stiftung%20arbeiten

Federal Ministry of Justice 2023, Works Constitution Act §§ 75 and 93, retrieved on 25.08.2023, https://www.gesetze-im-internet.de/betrvg/__75.html

HR-ROCKET 2023, Consideration of diversity in the creation of job advertisements, retrieved 25.08.2023; https://www.hr-rocket.com/diversity-recruiting/#einleitung-diversity-recruiting

Diversity Charter 2023, retrieved 24.08.2023, https://www.charta-der-vielfalt.de/fuerarbeitgebende/vielfaltsdimensionen/

Personalwirtschaft 2021, Diversity: How networks promote mutual understanding; accessed 20.08.2023, https://www.personalwirtschaft.de/news/recruiting/diversity-management-commerzbank-netzwerke-97102/25/

A world of diversity (2023), Network, accessed 24.08.2023, https://www.ewdv-diversity.de/ueber-uns/netzwerk

Issworld 2023, How recruiting with diversity and inclusion makes the world work better, retrieved 25.08.2023 https://www.issworld.com/de-de/insights/insights/cr-stories/how-hiring-for-diversity-and-inclusion-makes-the-world-work-better

Federal Anti-Discrimination Agency 2023, accessed 25.08.2023, https://www.antidiskriminierungsstelle.de/

Network Diversity 2023, Network Diversity at Universities, retrieved 26.08.2023, https://netzwerk-diversity.de/

Aktion Mensch 2022, Digitalization offers opportunities for people with disabilities, retrieved 26.08.23, 2023, https://www.aktion-mensch.de/inklusion/arbeit/zahlen-daten-fakten 2022

bagbbw 2023, Federal Association of Vocational Training Centers 2023, accessed 26.08.2023, https://www.bagbbw.de/

4.1.3 Recruitment policy that promotes Hyper Leadership

The equal treatment of people is enshrined in law. Article 3 of the Basic Law of the Federal Republic of Germany stipulates that all people are equal before the law. This is intended to prevent any form of discrimination. The text of the law states: "The aim of the law is to prevent or eliminate discrimination on the grounds of race or ethnic origin, gender, religion or belief, disability, age or sexual identity" (Federal Ministry of Justice 2022). The political debate on the concept of race is still ongoing (2023).

This law naturally includes employment relationships. But the reality is far from this, although studies have shown that diverse teams generate greater efficiency and higher turnover and profits. Leadership in management has also been proven to generate more innovation (JOIN 2022). The concept of establishing a diverse workforce not only helps to bring the idea of the law to life, it is ultimately also a contribution to a fairer world, which in this aspect has not yet been implemented even in advanced and democratic societies. An appropriately diverse workforce is nothing other than a reflection of society in the workplace context.

The majority of the workforce supports leadership in the workplace. In 2020, a Glassdoor survey revealed that 76% of employees and job seekers consider leadership to be an important factor in how a company is rated (JOIN 2022). On Glassdoor, former or current employees anonymously rate their company. Glassdoor has locations in America and Europe, including Hamburg.

The first step in establishing leadership appropriately in your own company is to analyze the current situation as accurately as possible. To do this, it is necessary to statistically evaluate the personnel data. This makes it necessary to assign individual people to different criteria. In order to clarify whether a shortage exists under certain aspects, the facts must be available. The assignment of male or female is comparatively simple. People who openly declare themselves to be "diverse" instead of a binary gender in company contacts are still rare. A great deal of sensitivity is required here. However, the first thing to keep in mind is whether employees with this characteristic should be recruited.

It is noticeable here that characteristics such as skin color, origin, disability and the like must be recorded in the personnel documents. It goes without saying that this is not a discriminatory approach, but necessary factual knowledge. There are now clear objectives, for example to include staff with a non-German cultural background to a greater extent. Such goals should be considered in terms of where they could also coincide with specific needs of the company. Is it also economically efficient if parts of the staff speak a certain language, are particularly familiar with a culture or another country, have a special skill (such as an autistic island talent) or know certain social circumstances from experience? Such factors are often not taken into account because leadership is not even considered from these perspectives. Of course, the level of analysis and development should be evaluated regularly.

The statistical evaluation provides a picture of what should be given priority in recruiting. Based on this, networking can begin and internal and external sources can be used. HR management often relies on using a resource once over and over again. This saves time and work. However, the recruitment of diverse talent in particular requires both more intensively than in conventional human resources management. In addition to targeted advertisements and job boards, several different job boards need to be used. A typical human characteristic is to always fall back on something that has worked before. However, as leadership involves several parameters, it is worth extending the commitment to several platforms.

When presenting your own company in the recruitment process, it is fundamentally important to make leadership visible and to do so authentically. Inclusive wording is paramount. All readers should feel addressed. A brief outline of the corporate culture is also helpful. This should make it clear that no one is excluded and that there are various offers. A holistic overview is therefore a good idea. It would be ideal if the employees had formed internal networks. For example, offers such as sports activities for all genders, remote working options, flexible working hours or variations in canteen food for different groups are worth mentioning. As many companies still find it strange when fathers take parental leave, this option is also worth mentioning as being welcome or already practiced.

One far-sighted way of integrating diverse talent is to build up a talent network. The company integrates this into its website. Visitors are invited to participate in the network. Invitations to events and, of course, the latest job advertisements can be found here. Public relations work can contribute to the expansion of the network. A company presence at job fairs, trade fairs or well-attended presentations is necessary for this. This gives participants the opportunity to register for the company network on the spot. It is important to remember data protection and ask for consent directly (Talention 2022).

Ideally, interested parties will receive a newsletter. In any case, they should have access to regular information. In this way, HR management keeps in touch with different people. The larger the number of participants, the greater the chance of finding diverse talent. Diverse people in particular often prefer to engage with a company in this way first. This gives them the confidence to apply. HR management maintains a good overview of potential applicants. A personal approach is much easier and more promising than without an existing contact.

One resource for diverse personnel management is a talent pool. This is a database containing the skills profiles of promising applicants. However, it can also include parts of the current workforce, e.g. in the event of staff redeployment or restructuring in the company. A talent pool can also be created for the sole purpose of recruiting diverse people. Networks of all kinds are one way of doing this. Basically, the aim is to get in touch with the people in question quickly and to be able to offer them a suitable position when the time comes. With regard to the data in the talent pool, it is important to note that leadership factors are recorded without being considered discriminatory characteristics.

The pool is expanded through dedicated public relations work. This includes internships and events. Offering internships makes it easier for various people to join a company. Above all, they are encouraged to apply for jobs when they experience leadership in the workplace. You can offer such opportunities on numerous platforms in addition to your own website. You can also contact various institutions specifically. For young people, universities, vocational schools and vocational training centers are also a good option here.

When making invitations, it is always important to remember that various people feel addressed. But autism centers are also a place to go, because autistic people in particular have difficulties fitting into a company straight away. Getting to know each other for the first time is a great help for them. Other options are cultural centers. Research relating to the region is useful. Internships can be completed at a specific workplace or in several departments. Here, HR management can provide guidance as required.

Invitations to events are also a good idea. An open day allows people to find out more without obligation. The diverse corporate culture should be clearly visible and tangible. There are many ideas, from diverse employees in the workplace to information in different languages and a varied culinary offering. Attractive materials that are available for job fairs can also be used.

The events also include events to mark special days. This could be a company anniversary, but also a summer party or an Advent bazaar. You can also look around in other cultures and search for an event there. This is a good idea if you want to strengthen cultural leadership. Or do you want to appeal to people with physical disabilities? Then organize a barrier-free day - e.g. with a wheelchair rally.

At each of these events, the offer to join the company network should be included. Each event has a multiplier effect because many people from the workforce mobilize members from their circle of friends and acquaintances. It is also an opportunity for recruitment to reach different target groups by providing information.

Literature

JOIN 2022, 13 steps for better diversity recruiting, accessed 31.08.2023,
https://join.com/de/recruitment-hr-blog/diversity-recruiting-strategie

Talention 2022, 7 reasons why you should have a Talent Network, retrieved
01.09.2023, https://www.talention.de/blog/7-gr%C3%BCnde-warum-sie-ein-talent-
network-haben-sollten

4.2 Selection process for talent

4.2.1 Avoiding prejudices and stereotypes

Prejudices and stereotypes serve two different thought patterns. Stereotypes are an expression of a generalization. The generalization provides a pattern on the basis of which one assesses other people. This applies in particular to people you meet for the first time. People are categorized on the basis of characteristics whose perennial and valid qualities are believed to be known. Such mechanisms exist all over the world. The classifications can help to assign perceptions and facilitate criteria for judgment. In this respect, they serve as an orientation aid in a diverse world. The problem is that they are judgmental attributions. Such stereotypes easily lead to the formation of opinions that are not justified in reality. If they become entrenched, they develop into prejudices. This is why stereotypes - which do not always have to be negative - often form the breeding ground and basis for prejudices, which in turn represent factually unfounded opinions. (Career Bible 2022)

Common stereotypes are: German thoroughness, Brazilian dancing talent, slowness in the civil service and the assertion that music is in the blood of people with black skin.

In social psychological literature, prejudice is defined as an attitude not only towards people and groups, but also towards objects and circumstances. It is not based on experience, but on generalizations (spektrum.de 2000). This definition can also be a positive attitude. In reality, however, prejudices often turn out to be negative attitudes. Examples of prejudices are that Swabian people are stingy and that Polish people steal more than average.

A study in the journal Science Advances is intended to show how quickly stereotypes can turn into prejudices and lead to concrete disadvantages. Based on the results of the 2018 PISA studies from 72 countries, it examined views on the factors of gifts and talents. Both were associated with men rather than women in almost all countries. In terms of self-reports, girls considered themselves less talented than boys did. This phenomenon was particularly evident in connection with performance. The high-achieving boys rated themselves as more talented overall than the high-achieving girls. This results in the problem that girls tend to perceive themselves as inadequate despite their skills and knowledge, while boys tend to overestimate themselves.

A surprising result at first glance showed that these different assessments were much more pronounced in economically and technically highly developed countries. Only the Saudi Arabian girls were more convinced that they had talents than the boys there. In all other countries, girls were far less likely than boys to believe that they were gifted and talented. One explanation for this could be that the tendency towards individualism is becoming more and more pronounced in more developed countries. In order to find one's way through the increasingly confusing multitude of individual phenomena, it helps to classify them into types. It makes sense to use familiar and frequently used classifications without reflection. One of these is the gender roles that have existed for centuries. (Profiling Institute 2022)

As even young people assess themselves in terms of their skills on a gender-specific basis, this attitude is also to be expected when applying for jobs. Similar basic attitudes of feeling less talented or untalented must be expected at least among some diverse people. It is therefore important to exercise particular caution when recruiting.

Personnel management can also be subject to unconscious attitudes based on stereotypes, even if they are not intentional. This is referred to as "unconscious bias", i.e. distorted perception in personnel recruitment. It is therefore a good idea for the relevant employees to reflect on their own disposition towards stereotypes and prejudices. There are hardly any people who are completely free of them. Anyone who identifies such attitudes in themselves is far from falling into categories such as sexist, racist or similar. It is important to realize which ideas exist and where they come from. This is the best way to counteract them. However, it would be a very tall order to consider them fully and always and not use any measures to help you be objective.

Some attitudes may be due to individual experience. Anyone who has observed women who can't park a few times quickly comes to the conclusion that all women can't park - a common stereotype. Even some women cultivate it. Anyone who has seen Turkish men fighting a few times quickly comes to the conclusion that all Turkish men are violent. The problem lies in the fact that such judgments are made on the basis of incorrect attributions. The fact that a person cannot park is tied to her gender as a woman. The fact that a man is a Turk is assumed to be the reason why he is violent. It is precisely this way of thinking that needs to be overcome. Incidentally, a single observation to the contrary would be enough to disprove the stereotype or prejudice. However, people often focus their perceptions on events that confirm their preconceived opinion.

Prejudices can be positive, which makes them more difficult to recognize. People tend to find others likeable and competent if they resemble them. This is known as the "mini-me effect". They are by no means discarded because they are judged negatively, but are taken into consideration because we sense a human affinity with them. The greatest risk of this prejudice is at the moment of first meeting. The widespread belief that "first impressions count" has a kernel of truth. Within seconds, we form an opinion based on our experiences and beliefs. This behavior is part of our genetic makeup. Our ancestors had to decide in a matter of seconds whether to flee, freeze or fight. Many studies show that men tend to prefer men, women tend to prefer women and tall people prefer tall people. Unconscious sympathies also arise with many other similarities, e.g. the same political views or the same sport. (Stellenanzeigen.de 2022)

The most widespread stereotypes and prejudices include the following views:

1. People with a different skin color and a different origin would be less competent

In addition to skin color, outward appearances such as clothing can also lead to discrimination. Other physical characteristics that often lead to discrimination due to incorrect assessments are height, build and voice. The taller, stronger or deeper they are, the more competence is assumed. As a rule, men have an advantage here.

2. People with disabilities could achieve less

It is often assumed that they are absent particularly often. Disabled people whose disability is visible are at a particular disadvantage here. People who use wheelchairs are more at risk of prejudice than those who have a transplanted organ.

3. Older employees would work less efficiently than younger ones

Statistics show that older employees are more likely to be disadvantaged by not being hired or dismissed due to their age.

If personnel management employees have dealt with the possibility of their own unconscious bias, they are well protected from being led by their first impression of a person at the interview. A consciously clear attitude also helps to avoid interrupting the interviewee prematurely and to let them finish speaking. The choice of words and the way they are expressed can counteract prejudices. This opportunity should be taken.

There are a number of helpful measures for remaining objective. These include the following.

- The talent pool comes into play from the point of view of avoiding prejudices. It should contain several people from the same "category" of diversity. Another characteristic of unconscious bias is that a single person with a particular characteristic is more likely to be rejected than if there were several with it. Examples include only one woman, one disabled person or one person from a different ethnic group.

- Objective methods provide a high guarantee of not suppressing diversity and remaining fair in the selection process. Anonymization is therefore a good option. CVs can also be easily anonymized using suitable software. Names, addresses and places of education are removed. As elite universities often trigger a positive prejudice, the names of universities can also be included. It is also possible to anonymize the information on gender and origin and remove the photo. (Diversity and Inclusion 2023)
- Anonymized written interviews can precede a job interview. They only include questions about knowledge and skills and not about personal circumstances. Some companies use such interviews instead of a job interview.

But ultimately, getting to know each other in person is essential. The same questions should therefore be asked of each person at the interview. This approach ensures neutrality. Objectivity is also promoted by the presence of more than one person at the interview. It is now quite common for 2 employees from HR management to attend. (Stellenanzeigen.de 2022).

There is a special feature to consider for people with disabilities if the application process is anonymous. While you can be well prepared for many outward appearances, there are phenomena with people with physical disabilities for which it is difficult to be prepared. Wheelchairs can be taken into account when mentally preparing for a job interview, but people in wheelchairs are also different. While some are relatively mobile, others need assistance. Pity, insecurity or rejection may be triggered by their appearance. In addition, there are disabilities whose nature cannot be predicted, which is particularly the case with deformities.

It should therefore be considered whether a job advertisement should include information such as "People with disabilities are expressly encouraged to apply". The public sector generally uses the wording "People with disabilities will be given preference if equally qualified". This satisfies the legal requirement to meet the employment quota for disabled people. A good solution here is also a talent pool that takes several disabled people into account.

There is no need to hide the fact that you are on the lookout for diverse talents in a job interview. This appreciation will please the candidates. At the same time, it is important that the existing skills and knowledge are right. No one should be hired just because they have a diverse attribute. However, no one should feel that they are being rejected because of their diversity. Clear information is therefore required about the inclusion of diverse people and also about fairness, appropriateness and objectivity.

After the interview, it is advisable to maintain appreciative contact. If it takes a long time to respond with a decision, this should be communicated. In the event of a rejection, the reasons for the rejection and the criteria that played a role should be explained. In the case of diverse individuals, it should be considered whether it makes sense to point out that leadership was not a reason for rejection. It should also be considered whether a rejected applicant should be moved to the talent pool.

Literature

Career Bible 2022, Stereotype: Definition, examples + tips, retrieved 09.09.2023, https://karrierebibel.de/stereotyp/

Spektrum.de 2000, Vorurteile (Bernd Six and Iris Six-Materna), retrieved 09.09.2023, https://www.spektrum.de/lexikon/psychologie/vorurteile/16528

Profiling Institute 2022, Gender stereotypes: Men are considered more talented, retrieved 09.09.2023, https://www.profiling-institut.de/geschlechter-stereotype/

Stellenanzeigen.de 2022, Unconscious Bias in Recruiting: How to overcome unconscious bias 2022, accessed 09.09.2023, https://www.stellenanzeigen.de/arbeitgeber/wecruit/unconscious-bias-im-recruiting-ueberwinden/#:~:text=Personaler%20m%C3%B6gen%20Menschen%2C%20die%20ihnen%20%C3%A4hnlich%20sind&text=Zahlreiche%20Studien%20belegen%2C%20dass%20M%C3%A4nner,seine%20Chancen%2C%20eingestellt%20zu%20werden

Diversity and inclusion 2023, Diversity and inclusion in recruitment: why you should pay attention, accessed 09.09.2023, https://www.surveymonkey.de/mp/diversity-recruiting/.

4.2.2 Assessment of Skills and Potential

When recruiting, the goal for a company is always to find the right employees for a position, i.e. the right person in the right place. It is important to ensure that diversity is taken into account. At the same time, a leadership characteristic alone should not be the decisive criterion. This would cause a lot of resentment in the workforce - even if it already contains diverse talents. Skills and knowledge should be consistent. Of course there are non-diverse people in the talent pool. It's about balance and not obsessive selection. This is just as important as avoiding unconscious bias. This should be mentioned for the sake of completeness.

In addition to professional qualifications, personal skills, also known as soft skills or key qualifications, also play a role when filling vacancies. A distinction can be made between five areas (Business Administration Learning 2023).

1. Social skills enable a person to interact appropriately

In both everyday and professional situations, it is necessary to communicate appropriately, both verbally and non-verbally. This area of competence also includes the ability to cooperate with colleagues, be team-oriented and deal constructively with conflicts. It also includes the ability to accept criticism and to express it appropriately.

2. Self-competence reflects a person's individual personal attitude, which naturally also has an impact in the professional environment

It is also referred to as empowerment. It is both the willingness and the ability to face the challenges of professional (and private) life and to deal with them appropriately. It is demonstrated by using one's own development opportunities and talents. This includes being able to act independently and responsibly and having healthy self-confidence. Your own value system is also located here. Religious and ideological convictions play a role here.

3. Methodological competence is the ability to tackle tasks and challenges in a meaningful way

The criteria here are the means by which solutions are planned and how the planning is implemented.

4. Media literacy is about the ability to use contemporary communication channels and media appropriately

It must be possible to create presentations using the usual, current means. Decision-making skills, the ability to reflect and problem-solving skills are required for implementation.

5. Action competence is about reacting appropriately in specific situations

Unplanned situations often occur in operational practice, which is why this competence is of great importance. This ability is essential in order to deliver the required performance according to the job description. Employees are also expected to actively take responsibility for their tasks.

There are overlaps in the classification of skills, and some skills can be categorized in different areas. Some soft skills are often in demand. These include motivation, reliability, organizational skills and time management. If you have to deal with customers, you should also have negotiating skills and customer orientation as well as the appropriate rhetorical skills. Some companies already count intercultural competence as a soft skill.

With regard to leadership, it should be noted that other cultures and ethnic groups have different ideas about some soft skills. In German companies, punctuality is generally regarded as a sought-after skill. This is different in other countries. However, it must be said that there is a trend towards practicing the division of core and functional working hours, so that showing up on time (or rather a little earlier) is less and less required. Other skills can also be assessed very differently for different people. There is a danger here of expecting different skills from different people or ascribing them to them by default. Examples include helpfulness, assertiveness and resilience. They are among those that are - even unconsciously - easily assigned to specific genders.

Men and women can ascribe a characteristic to themselves (or demand that they display it). However, there may also be different expectations of the male and female genders. The same problem can occur with people from other countries. There is a danger of unconsciously expecting less assertiveness and more helpfulness, for example.

When it comes to resilience, people with disabilities often run the risk of being underestimated. One example is people on the autism spectrum. Many of them have difficulty processing sounds, light and/or smells as easily as people without this disability (Autism Culture 2023). This is why they often cannot find a job. Help is available, ranging from headphones and low-noise or low-light rooms to the organization of working hours in which there is less stimulation. Once the problem has been solved, people perform as required. Performance is often high because they have the ability to focus strongly.

When it comes to the soft skills required, it is important that they match the job. If you are expected to perform individually, you do not need to be a strong team player. If you are primarily involved with numbers, you do not need to be particularly creative.

In order to avoid unconscious evaluations that associate certain soft skills with certain groups of people by attributing or denying them, it is advisable to use a personality test. This should ideally not be used as a pre-selection tool, but only in connection with the job interviews. A test is a supplementary module for reaching a decision. No one should be excluded on this basis. Rather, the test should be used to better assess the people in question. It is primarily about understanding them and less about making an assessment (Haufe.de 2023). Especially when it comes to soft skills, it is not advisable to draw up a wish list and compare it with the results of the test. The misunderstandings could be too great.

Regarding personality tests, it is important to select one that is as objective as possible. If applicants are only asked to tick yes/no answers, there is a greater risk of falsification. There are tests that take a more differentiated approach. They present statements that are to be evaluated in stages from "completely true" to "not true at all" (e.g. the "Bochum Inventory for Job-Related Personality Description").

In order to remain unbiased when selecting future employees, it is advisable to draw up a shortlist. It is a model for ensuring equal opportunities as far as possible. In addition, HR management also gains a clear idea of what they are looking for. What exactly is required for the position is noted on this list. These are the professional qualifications and the most important soft skills. Any characteristics relating to the person (origin, age, gender, which university, etc.) are disregarded. Companies that include personal criteria on their shortlist are therefore already acting in a discriminatory manner. The shortlist serves as a selection tool for incoming applications with the aim of finding staff with the right skills and incorporating leadership.

A shortlisting scorecard table can be developed from the shortlist. This lists the desired factors and weights them using a points system. The factors from the application documents are then compared. For example, if experience in a specific field is desired, the applicant will receive more points if they have more experience. (Join 2021).

If you only use education and professional experience as criteria for qualification in shortlisting, you run the risk of exclusion. Different training courses in different countries can turn out very differently. It is also possible to acquire skills with experience.

If an assessment center is used, the people conducting it should definitely have undergone leadership training. When using software and artificial intelligence, there is a risk of errors. Above all, applicants with good aptitude will fall out if they do not fit into the usual training and career scheme. It is essential to carry out human checks on the results.

Literature

Learning business administration 2023, key qualification, accessed 15.09.2023, https://www.betriebswirtschaft-lernen.net/erklaerung/schluesselqualifikation/?utm_content=cmp-true

Autism Culture 2023, Autism and Perception, retrieved 15.09.2023, https://autismus-kultur.de/wahrnehmung-autistischer-menschen/?utm_content=cmp-true

Haufe.de 2023, Dr. Roland Franke: Five tips for personnel selection with personality tests, retrieved 15.09.2023, https://www.haufe.de/personal/hr-management/recruiting-personalauswahl-mit-persoenlichkeitstests_80_544590.html

Join 2021, Fair shortlisting made easy, accessed 17.09.2023, https://join.com/de/recruitment-hr-blog/faires-shortlisting-leicht-gemacht.

5 Inspiring talent

An inclusive corporate culture must come from the management. It should actively develop and maintain an appreciative and trusting working atmosphere. Supporting measures should be used to promote leadership. These include mentoring and coaching. They are used for personnel development, from skills development to career planning.

5.1 Creating an inclusive corporate culture

5.1.1 Promotion of an open and respectful work environment

A company always has a corporate culture. However, it may not consciously live it or question it. A culture is then often cultivated that is not characterized by leadership. Many companies develop a corporate philosophy once and then display it in their reception area. However, this does not guarantee that they will act accordingly. A good corporate culture requires reflection and conscious action. It largely harmonizes its ideals and its actions.

Promoting an open and respectful working environment involves factors that not only have an internal impact, but also an external one. Those who live leadership in their day-to-day work also show this as a matter of course in their public relations work. This is another reason why diverse employees who carry out their work should be depicted on the website, be it a wheelchair-bound person in front of a PC or an elderly person at reception. They should also be included in media work, from the company's own newsletter to newspaper articles. It is important that they are presented as employees as a matter of course. An emphasis such as "We also employ diverse people" can prove counterproductive. Emphasizing "being different" in particular can easily be seen as disrespect.

Successful inclusion of diverse people means no longer focusing on leadership or not measuring people against it. If you put them in the foreground, you provoke the diverse factor to be seen as the cause of their professional behavior. Making this connection is the basis for prejudices and stereotypes. Someone does something well, badly or mediocre because they have certain knowledge and skills and not because they are diverse. As a corporate culture, responsible leadership management strives to ensure that all employees view leadership as a matter of course (Diversity Charter 2023) and also demonstrate this attitude to the outside world.

If they are naturally included in the representation of the company, this strengthens the diverse talents. It promotes their perception and their experience that they are treated openly, without prejudice and respectfully. This is why the way a company presents itself to outsiders is also part of the working environment. This is often underestimated. Employees also talk about their work in a non-professional environment. They should be able to identify with the company and refer to the website and other media with a good feeling.

When various employees read the latest newsletter, this has an impact on their identification with the company. If they feel appropriately represented, this strengthens a respectful working environment. Diverse employees whose diversity is not outwardly visible, but who are included, also feel seen.

Of course, there are also effects among non-diverse employees. They experience that the corporate culture makes the commitment to leadership visible. The aim is also to ensure that they do not get the impression that diverse people are represented more strongly because they bring their own specific attributes to the table. Of course, non-diverse employees must always be reflected in the company's representation. A good basis is to use the figures from HR management as a guide and derive a certain proportionality from them. For example, there are companies that employ many people with disabilities. It is then appropriate to represent them in the public relations work in an appropriate proportion.

Within internal communication, it is advisable to report on successes from time to time, especially from teams with diverse members. Small stories that tell something about the accomplishment of a specific task not only lead to easy-to-read information, but also to an open working atmosphere. The natural interaction in the workplace during such presentations both demonstrates and promotes an open working environment.

Internally, the aim is still to offer all employees a respectful working environment. Disabled people are of course provided with the necessary aids such as height-adjustable desks or special keyboards. However, non-disabled employees also appreciate a well-equipped workplace. Under no circumstances should a diverse person be given the impression that they are at a disadvantage. Equally, this impression should not be given to non-diverse people either. For example, ergonomic workplace design should not be limited to older employees or those with disabilities.

Ideally, employees respect each other. Their communication with each other is an important component that contributes to a sense of well-being in the workplace. It is important to remember that people come together who may prioritize completely different values in their private lives. No one should be criticized for this. Leadership can start with whether someone has children or not. Different beliefs, world views, religions and social circumstances such as the type of home, hobbies and circle of friends come together.

The aesthetic of the individual working environment (and of course the entire spatial design) should not make other employees feel irritated or discredited. Therefore, such images, slogans and texts should be avoided at all workplaces. At the same time, attributes, behaviors and statements should be respected as long as they do not demean others. If someone is enthusiastic about a certain sports club, wears a certain hairstyle or does not speak perfect German, for example, these are not factors that affect other employees. Respectful communication is particularly important in teamwork. At the same time, all employees should have the impression that respect runs through all levels of the hierarchy. Cleaning staff should be treated with the same respect as management. Flat hierarchies often contribute to this attitude.

Literature

*Diversity Charter 2023, Future factor diversity, accessed 22.09.2023,
https://www.charta-der-
vielfalt.de/fileadmin/user_upload/Studien_Publikationen_Charta/Charta_der_Vielfa
lt_-_KMU-Brosch%C3%BCre_2020.pdf.*

5.1.2 Appreciation of Hyper Leadership and individuality

The feeling of being valued plays a major role in everyday working life. On the one hand, it is about acceptance in terms of performance. No one should be considered less capable because they are diverse. As soon as such a prejudiced attitude is the case, performance is assessed incorrectly, i.e. too low. Secondly, it is about valuing personality. With diverse people, in particular, it is important to accept them in their entirety and to convey this attitude to them. The minimum level is not to perceive them in a judgmental way.

This means maintaining an open attitude towards other people, even if your own values do not coincide with their views or actions. In everyday working life, it is necessary to recognize and respect other employees as individuals. (Diversity Charter 2023).

This also includes the awareness that diversity manifests itself in various forms of individuality. It is precisely this fact that results in companies finding more solutions and productivity. The company should always point this out, especially internally. At the same time, the various individuals should show appreciation for each other so that cooperation remains as conflict-free as possible.

It must always be borne in mind that many people who do not fall into the "diverse" category can also have a very individual personality with unusual characteristics. They may also need special conditions. For example, there are people who are not team players or are particularly sensitive to noise.

In practice, appreciation is promoted by having as many employees as possible in contact with each other (Young Heart Agency 2021). At work, it is possible to set up working groups on various topics. It is not a problem to ensure a diverse composition. In routine work, the focus is naturally on which skills are required. But here, too, you can evaluate from the point of view of diversity and, based on this, change the composition of a department/team.

Familiarizing new employees with diversity from the outset strengthens the inclusive atmosphere, regardless of whether the newcomers themselves are diverse talents or not. Particularly when first getting to know each other, differences are often noticeable in terms of choice of words and behavior. Not every unexpected or non-conformist action or statement is based on diversity. Many habits are simply individual and just take some getting used to.

Another measure in this context is the regular cross-departmental introduction of new employees to each other. This is also where diverse and non-diverse people meet, all of whom have one thing in common, namely that they belong to the group of the newest employees in the company.

The department or team itself should organize an introductory event for the new employees. This should take place to a manageable extent, be it in the form of a coffee round scheduled before the first team meeting or a snack at a suitable time. In any case, this introductory round should be part of working hours.

A checklist is useful for personnel management. For example, the participants also introduce themselves in their native language or report on a cultural rite. Depending on the time of year, Easter, Christmas and holidays from other cultural and religious backgrounds may be suitable. And/or everyone talks about their hobbies. Many points are possible here. In any case, similarities will be recognized across the boundaries of diversity. After all, people celebrate similar occasions and have similar ways of making their leisure time meaningful. Such gatherings not only strengthen the basis for working together; they also promote mutual appreciation.

5.1.3 Building a culture of trust and cooperation

Trust is one of the most important feelings in human life. It conveys the feeling of having support. Basic trust refers to the fact that people believe they are protected by a higher power or fate. Even when they find themselves in difficult situations, they assume that everything has a purpose and will turn out well. Trust is just as important in interpersonal relationships because it involves the conviction of having the support of other people.

Trust also has a future-related aspect. If other people's actions in the future are difficult to predict, this triggers uncertainty and possibly anxiety. People who seems to be confident in their actions might not be so dependent on trust signals received from others. But sooner or later, people find themselves in situations in which they lack this certainty. This is particularly true for diverse people.

Confidence influences the ability to act. People who have confidence literally trust themselves to do something, and are able to make their own choices, free from fear, when faced with complex tasks requiring different solutions. In particular, the experience of having one's own decisions corrected by others - e.g. by superiors - without negative consequences promotes confidence. Correcting a decision is an objective measure. A negative consequence would be reproach or embarrassment.

However, having trust also makes you vulnerable. If it is broken and one's own decision is evaluated negatively, for example, this affects the person - perhaps even severely. "Trust implies a risky choice, whereby the risk lies in having to bear negative personal consequences if trust is destroyed" (Spektrum 2000).

In everyday working life, it is important that there is an atmosphere of trust. Employees should feel that they can count on support both in their routine work and in special tasks and difficult situations. This is not just a moral issue. A lack of trust impairs the individual's ability to act. It also makes the company less capable of acting and, as a result, less productive and less creative in finding solutions.

As soon as people feel excluded, their self-esteem dwindles along with their confidence, and with it their creative power. This applies to both private and professional contexts. That is why it is particularly important to show trust in various people. They have often not been able to build up this feeling sufficiently or have at least partially lost it in the course of their experiences.

A company should be underpinned by a corporate culture that fosters trust, both within the hierarchically equal employees and across hierarchical boundaries, right down to the relationship between top management and employees at lower levels. This is the best basis for good cooperation.

The culture cultivated in a company is both visible and tangible, even for outsiders. It is important to distinguish between three levels. The organizational psychologist Edgar Schein made the following classification (Missionsustainable 2021):

On the visible and perceptible level, the most important aspects are the language conventions, the organizational structure and the resulting processes, the layout of the premises and the dress code. This also includes internal networks and technological equipment.

These structures are based on certain values and norms. These represent the deeper, invisible level of the lived culture. Companies make these more or less public. Conscious decisions are often displayed for all to see, both virtually on the website and, for example, in the entrance area on site. Christian institutions will always point out the factors that make up a Christian image of humanity, e.g. love of neighbor. Inclusive organizations should mention leadership as a value. Standards also belong to this level, e.g. complaints and quality management. Furthermore, there can be written declarations, e.g. defined rules of conduct that apply in the company. Explicit commitments are also possible for fundamental attitudes relating to values and standards. One example is the CSR guidelines (CSR Directive 2023). Binding for several hundred large companies as well as banks and insurance companies since 2017, these must set out environmental and social factors. Examples include concepts for employee rights and measures against corruption.

Below this level lies the deepest layer. It contains the unconscious fundamental attitudes. These have a strong influence on how a corporate culture is lived. The actual, real design does not always have to match what is envisaged in the statutes and concepts. These attitudes are often not questioned. They relate, for example, to individual ideas about communication within the same or different hierarchical levels, to the application of ideas about different gender roles or the question of who works how much overtime.

In a company that values leadership and wants to treat diverse people without prejudice, it is important to reach this deep layer. Diverse factors must not be used to exclude employees in a group or even prevent them from progressing. It is therefore important to treat leadership as a matter of course. This is the way to cultivate a diverse corporate culture at all levels. Mutual trust can then be established and good cooperation within the immediate working environment as well as across hierarchical boundaries can be built and maintained.

5.2 Leaders as a source of inspiration

5.2.1 Authentic and empathic leadership

The first point that needs to be clarified at management level is that leadership is fundamentally desirable. If the management team consists of several people and only one or a minority is committed to employing diverse people, the conditions are poor. The first step is to discuss this issue, highlight the benefits of leadership in terms of business profit and evaluate the company's overall situation. Prioritizing economic factors is a legitimate measure. Not all managers have to be convinced of all aspects. Their own values may be at odds with various individual factors. It is always difficult to tackle deeply rooted ideas in one's own personality structure. Of course, this also applies to senior managers. But management should agree not only to tolerate leadership, but also to value and promote it.

In detail, the various areas of responsibility can be skillfully distributed among different heads. Managers also have a family and a circle of friends who share certain values and norms. They are also at risk of cultivating unconscious bias. And they also have different skills in terms of communication and organizational talent. They should be assigned to an area of responsibility that they can represent. This includes an open and honest discussion within the management team.

At the hierarchical levels below management, there may always be situations where leadership management does not work. However, it is essential that all senior employees lead as authentically and empathetically as the managers do. In order to achieve this, the management can take a number of measures for the other management levels.

1. She issues a handout with arguments in favor of leadership. This gives everyone something concrete to work with. It is best to present it to the workforce in a meeting. Here, too, there is no need to hide the fact that many companies with leadership have achieved good economic success.

2. She gets an idea of where she can find supportive employees in the company and integrates them better into the relevant structures.

3. It is putting together a team to launch diversity-related projects (Future Factor Diversity 2023).

70 percent of human resources professionals in the field of recruitment state that obstacles to recruiting diverse employees come from the management level. The problem does not necessarily lie in the fact that prejudices prevail here. Rather, managers often lack the courage to break new ground (Diversity and Inclusion 2023).

The management team should have a clear action plan on how to integrate Hyper Leadership into the company, build it up and maintain an appropriate level. This requires regular evaluations. Cooperation with the HR department is essential. It is necessary to define which areas are to be staffed and how. This can also be small-scale, e.g. bringing more people with disabilities into contact with customers or more women into the operational area. The approaches are of course different everywhere and must be worked out with empirical data. At the same time, they must be feasible.

All managers should support this action plan in principle. It should always be questioned whether quantitative votes in the management team are the appropriate instrument when it comes to important issues such as leadership. It is also often appropriate for managers to take advantage of coaching or supervision. Supervision professionally guides self-reflection processes and ensures that they are positive. It also serves to set clear objectives. Supervision is best carried out with the help of external specialists.

It is precisely experiences like these that lead to not only propagating one's own corporate culture, but also representing and living it authentically and empathetically. Every single encounter with managers is a special situation for employees. Representatives of higher hierarchical levels should always embody the philosophy that all members of the workforce are equally welcome and that their personalities are seen and respected.

The public relations department is often set up as a staff unit. Close communication with the management is then a given. The employees in this department are constantly challenged to make leadership visible both internally and externally and at the same time to present it as a matter of course. This can sometimes be a balancing act. It is important that employees are empathetic in their words and images. Their statements and presentations should be considered authentic when it comes to the inclusion of diverse people.

Of course, management is at its most authentic when there are diverse people in its ranks. Authenticity and empathy are therefore just as important within the management level as they are towards the workforce.

However, it should not be underestimated that such roles are not always easy for diverse employees. As long as leadership has not yet become a matter of course, they always run the risk of being criticized in their decisions, especially under the criterion of leadership. It is often easy to accuse them of not being strict enough or too caring with regard to other diverse people.

Employees should always be able to rely on the distribution of tasks being correct and unpleasant tasks being shared equally between all shoulders. Access to resources should also be fair. However, if this is not always the case for all employees, the leadership factor does not always have to be the cause. Objectivity is required when looking at things that need to be changed. leadership is not always the key issue.

5.2.2 Promoting innovation and creativity

Promoting innovation and creativity is a fundamental tool for increasing a company's overall productivity. Many companies underestimate this factor, expecting only routine tasks from their employees and only trusting specialists with progressive ideas.

How can management promote factors that stand out from the same everyday activities? There are selective and longer-term measures for this.

One option is to organize a workshop. This is usually a welcome change for employees anyway. There are numerous possibilities for suitable tasks. It should be noted that the focus in this context is on the enjoyment of the activities, which lead to new insights and increased motivation. The aim of such a workshop should not be to find a solution to a specific, small-scale operational problem. Rather, the focus should be on tasks that leave a certain amount of leeway.

Employees should be able to experience finding solutions by unleashing their creativity. This results in approaches that reveal different and possibly more far-reaching skills than those required in day-to-day routine work. Diverse people can reveal skills that are related to their leadership. This is an important experience for all employees. It is possible to include tasks that require the skills of diverse people. This could be the special memory skills of someone with Asperger's syndrome, the speed or transportation capacity of someone who uses an (e)-wheelchair, special cultural or ethnic knowledge or the vast experience of older employees. This calls for the expertise of an experienced coach who should be external but well prepared by HR management.

Group work is essential in such a workshop, as is changing the composition of the group. The experience of having arrived at surprising and satisfying solutions together has an impact on the motivation to allow creativity to flow into operational circumstances. This always presupposes that managers encourage such processes. Middle and lower management levels in particular should consciously set them in motion and use creativity-promoting methods, e.g. brainstorming, on a regular basis.

Workshops are also a good way of encouraging creativity, especially among senior employees, and of eliciting innovative ideas.

Another selective means is to hold a competition within the company. There are plenty of topics for this. Redesigning a hallway - with photos, for example - writing a report for the newsletter or suggesting a new recipe for the canteen are examples.

One longer-term management measure that promotes innovation and creativity concerns the composition of teams. The formation of cross-teams has proven to be suitable (Future Factor Diversity 2023). This involves two employees working together in a team of two. One person differs from the other in terms of a diverse characteristic. (Both can also be diverse or both non-diverse, but the inclusion of diverse people would not be addressed as thoroughly). Each person spends part of their working time observing and, if possible, participating in the workplace of the other. The completely new perspective on a routine work process often releases creative ideas as well as constructive criticism, naturally from both participants. This can lead to improvements.

There are companies that practice such cross-over across company boundaries together with partner companies. Especially when diverse people are involved, this not only promotes innovative and creative processes, but also the inclusion of diverse talents.

Managers can also form working groups in which a task is to be worked on across departments or disciplines. Such challenges often show how creatively a group, and in particular a diverse team, can work. Examples include organizing a company party and replanning food offerings in the canteen. New or restructured operational processes of all kinds are also suitable projects. The introduction or supervision of quality or complaints management is usually a working group topic, even if there is a person with primary responsibility. The involvement of various employees is essential for these issues.

In principle, management should never miss an opportunity to point out the creative and innovative aspects that contributed to this constructive development when a change is made that is important or affects all or the majority of employees. In such situations, it would be good to be able to show how employees and, above all, diverse talents were involved.

5.2.3 Career development and promotion opportunities

In the context of career opportunities for women, there is the term "glass ceiling". It means that although there are no objective reasons why women should not get into higher management positions, they still do not make it. This may still be partly due to a society's effect upon women: This can lead to little confidence in themselves, like to let others take the lead or, when in doubt, prioritize family work, leaving less time for gainful employment. But it is also still due to the fact that there is no parity in management positions. Far fewer women than men get further up the career ladder.

On May 15, 2015, a law came into force that provides for the equal participation of women and men in management positions, both in the private sector and in the public sector. To this end, it stipulated a proportion of 30% of the underrepresented gender (in real terms, women) from 2016. (Bmfsfj 2023). In 2022, however, the average proportion of women in Germany was 24.1% (International Women's Day 2022).

If it is already difficult to get women, who make up around half the population, into management positions, it is even more difficult for diverse people who are objectively in the minority. Accordingly, many companies shy away from considering diverse talents for promotion opportunities or do not even include them in their considerations.

It often requires a conscious decision to observe and assess diverse people solely on the basis of their skills and knowledge in order to give them equal opportunities. If the company carries out regular appraisals, this provides a tool for accessing data when it comes to promotion. Especially when it comes to promotion opportunities, it is important that managers reflect on any unconscious biases or stereotypes they may have and set clear and objective criteria for promotion.

A shortlist is well suited for this purpose and can be used during the selection process for new employees. The criteria are listed in a table and weighted according to a points system. The criteria should be critically examined to determine whether diversity could put a person at a disadvantage. For example, in some cultures it is customary to maintain friendly contact within the team. However, this is not synonymous with a lack of distance.

A management team that values diversity acts in an exemplary and authentic manner when it includes diverse talents in promotion processes. This opportunity should be taken for granted in the working environment. All measures and behaviors that regard and treat diverse people as natural employees and at the same time encourage possible exclusion are supportive. If diverse people move up within the company, it should not be said that they only got the job because of leadership, nor that they are not up to it because of diverse characteristics. At the same time, the situation can also arise in which a certain skill has to do with a person's leadership. In this case, however, the ability is the deciding factor. At the same time, diverse managers must ensure that they remain objective in their dealings with all subordinates. The appointment of new managers should always be communicated at least internally. Possibilities include the intranet, newsletters or meetings. Externally, newsletters and the website are also available. The local press can also report.

In principle, communication between management and employees should be characterized by trust as well as a shared conviction that performance is required. If there are opportunities for promotion, all employees should know the criteria for this. Companies that consciously implement leadership often have flat hierarchies. In this respect, such situations occur less frequently. However, it can happen more often that organizational tasks such as leading working groups have to be taken on. Here, management should be careful to ensure that diverse talents are included.

Highlighting career development and promotion opportunities is already a good point during interviews and job interviews. There are companies that ask younger women what their family plans are before hiring them, signaling that they do not consider children and a career to be compatible for women. This can make various people all the more insecure when they want to move up. If diverse people already hold important positions in the company, this is always a reassuring factor for newcomers, even if they themselves are not aiming for advancement.

5.3 Mentoring and coaching

5.3.1 The importance of mentoring programs

Alongside coaching, mentoring is becoming increasingly important in professional life. This method is also well suited for use in companies with diverse employees.

The word "mentor" comes from Latin and means artist. Today, however, "mentor" is understood to mean a teacher, even if they have nothing to do with the school. Rather, they are professionals. With their specific knowledge and extensive experience, they support people who are at the beginning of their careers. In principle, this is a sensible approach within a company. Newcomers are "mentored" for a while by individual well-integrated employees. This involves showing them different ways and/or the best way to complete tasks. Advice of all kinds is also provided. First and foremost, the aim is to achieve optimum mastery of the subject area. Nevertheless, the collaboration usually results in a personal relationship between mentor and mentee.

Mentoring programs primarily serve companies as a personnel development tool and also as career support (Mentoring 2021). They are particularly good for various people in the initial phase of their employment with the company, and also later on if they are suitable talents for promotion within the company. There are companies that support new employees from the outset with a view to promotion.

Mentoring for diverse employees must always consider and include the leadership factor. Both for diverse career starters and for diverse people who are to be given or have recently been given managerial positions, priority should be given to strengthening professional competence. This reduces the risk of discrimination. Those who feel confident in their specialist area and in their routine work are well armed against possible devaluations.

However, a mentoring program for diverse people should also include soft skills such as communication skills and work techniques. Social skills are also an issue. Further development in mastering operational tasks always goes hand in hand with personal development. It is therefore very important that mentor and mentee understand each other - especially when it comes to diverse mentees. A general goal is for mentees to feel comfortable in their role as an employee, to see a clear path ahead of them in the company and to have the self-confidence to follow it, regardless of whether they have aspirations for promotion or not.

A company can purchase an external mentoring service. However, in many cases it makes sense to use an internal mentoring program. This can be tailored to different employees. Mentors should have the appropriate sensitivity. Those involved in the mentoring process should be aware that both sides benefit from it. Mentors also learn a lot and develop their skills, for example in structured thinking and in the area of training. Furthermore, there will always be situations in which they themselves learn new technical skills, in many cases primarily in the digital field.

Mentoring is based on support over a longer period of time. Know-how is an essential component. Mentoring does not focus on just one aspect of the workplace. It aims at a positive development that affects various skills and knowledge.

Reverse mentoring is also an option for a diverse workforce (Future Factor Diversity 2023). This involves bringing together employees from different hierarchical levels. The focus here is on changing perspectives. The participants meet at eye level. Such programs are also appropriate to promote understanding between the genders and, of course, between one gender and people who are LGBTQIA+.

For the inclusion of women, one example of mentoring programs is that older male employees exchange ideas with younger female managers. The meeting takes place under the question: What can be learned from each other? It is not about showing that one is better than the other. It's about accepting differences and being open to the advantages that the other person brings with their way of leading. It is always a good idea to choose external mentors for such processes, as reverse mentoring involves two mentees who should not be left alone. External mentors are objective and can guide the process impartially. In a similar way, mentoring can also be carried out for diverse employees together with non-diverse employees.

In principle, groups can also be accompanied by a mentoring program, e.g. senior employees, teams or working groups.

Every type of mentoring requires mentees to contribute constructively to the process. Self-reflection is part of this and is encouraged during the process. Of course, this applies to non-diverse people as well as diverse people.

5.3.2 Coaching to promote professional development

Both mentoring and coaching are methods that managers are increasingly using to bring employees and the company together. They are often used when university graduates are offered their first job. However, they are also used for part-time employees without a degree (Diversity Coaching 2023).

In principle, both the management and the various people themselves can be coached. Groups can also be coached, for example departments. There is also the option of project-related coaching. In this case, the coaches accompany the project team members during the project. In the context of diversity, it is always important that diverse people are or remain well included. The method can therefore be used pragmatically.

Management is very important in that it must be convinced that leadership is desirable and that diverse talents are actively recruited. As long as there are still inhibiting reservations at management level, the coaching of managers takes priority. However, if leadership is a clear attitude that is both given appropriate importance in the mission statement and implemented in an exemplary manner in practice, it may make sense to coach diverse talents in order to strengthen their subjective perception of being a valuable member of the company. Groups should be coached if there are doubts as to whether their diverse members are sufficiently included.

Wherever coaching takes place, the company ultimately hopes to optimize the overall performance of the company. Internal company factors that make up this performance and can be promoted well through coaching are, above all, a good working atmosphere, the courage to be creative, motivation and employee identification with the company. Coaching can also reduce employee turnover. Such measures, which also include the development of personality, always aim to ensure the positive development of both the coached employees and the company as a whole. Even if the positive impact on the company is indirect, coaching should always result in a win-win situation for both the employer and the employee.

Coaching is a counseling method. In contrast to mentoring, it has a clearly defined goal. It can relate to technical content as well as to a specific situation in the workplace or a group dynamic process. Coaching does not establish a long-term personal relationship. The coach remains neutral towards the coachee, but critically questions behaviors and processes (Mentoring 2023). A set goal is to be achieved.

When coaching a management team, one goal can be to promote and accept leadership more consciously. In concrete terms, this would manifest itself in an action, such as greater inclusion in the external presentation or the revision of checklists in personnel management. In the case of an individual person, it may mean that they should be prepared for a managerial position, but do not feel confident enough to take it on because of their leadership, for example. In this case, the goal would be achieved if she accepts the position.

Coaching takes place at eye level. In the case of a group, it can be about reducing resentment towards leadership. The coaching would then aim to optimally include the diverse person(s). Success could be demonstrated by employees refraining from or consciously using certain language or behavior. It often makes sense to schedule a later time for reflection after the end of the coaching process, in which the development is verbalized and evaluated.

A coach does not give direction but knows various methods to reach a goal. They do not offer solutions, but rather ways for employees to find their own solutions. It is essential that the coachees are willing to self-reflect. Those who are accompanied by a coach find their own personal path. This applies not only to individuals, but also to groups. Group dynamic processes change the attitude of each individual member. Just like mentoring, coaching is only meaningful and successful if the coachees participate voluntarily.

Typical goals for coaching are (Mentoring 2021):

- the assessment and development of personal skills (with regard to a specific goal)
- Improving leadership quality
- Stress and time management (e.g. with regard to daily routine work)
- Dealing with a specific conflict (between two or more people)
- Formation of a new team
- Implementation of a specific project
- Inclusion of new employees

With regard to Hyper Leadership, the focus of coaching is always on ensuring that diverse talents are treated fairly and equally. Mentoring and coaching can use some of the same communication strategies. They can also merge into one another. For example, a mentoring program can end and be followed by coaching. Both methods have proven successful in practice.

5.3.3 Self-reflection and goal setting

Both mentoring programs and coaching are valuable support for diverse talents. They already serve the purpose of self-reflection and the pursuit of a goal. However, they are limited in time and not all diverse employees can generally take part in such measures. However, no diverse talent should fall by the wayside in the operational process. It is important to support all diverse employees in their self-reflection and goal setting.

Self-reflection includes thinking about one's own personal influences, one's own socialization process, one's own actions and one's own development opportunities (Erwachsenenbildung 2013). This means that professional self-reflection also involves large parts of the overall and therefore also the "private" personality. Accordingly, company-related discussions should also be conducted carefully and sensitively. Nevertheless, communication is the key to strengthening diverse talents in companies.

One possibility, which also includes the individual objectives of various people, is appraisal interviews or personnel development interviews. Many companies hold such meetings on a regular basis. In this context, diverse employees can be individually strengthened. If there are skills and knowledge that are related to leadership, this is a good opportunity to highlight this. At the same time, it should also be discussed how diverse employees feel well included and where they still see disadvantages for themselves. Appreciation from superiors in particular strengthens diverse talents. In such a discussion, socialization processes and personal experiences can also be named, for example as the cause of fears or impairments. In this way, it often becomes clear that leadership is not an obstacle to stringently pursuing a particular professional objective.

Another option is to hold regular discussions with a person who deals with the topic of leadership on a full-time basis. This could be an equal opportunities officer. Here, too, it is very important not to meet spontaneously, but regularly within consistent time frames. The topics of self-reflection and goal setting are generally suitable for inclusion on the agenda.

A confidential atmosphere is also important here. Diverse people have often had (and still have) experiences since childhood that differ considerably from those of non-diverse people. It is often good to verbalize them. Through such awareness-raising processes, diverse talents recognize connections to any resentment they experience. This helps them to better differentiate themselves from them and to confront them communicatively.

At the same time, diverse employees should always be told where their Hyper Leadership has contributed to a positive development, be it in a one-off situation or in a long-term matter. Confidential discussions are well suited for this purpose, as they allow different means of communication to be used than in the presence of other employees. Hyper Leadership can be discussed here in an unobserved and focused manner.

The respective managers can have a positive influence on various employees in their daily routine work as well as when working in working groups. Individual feedback is always possible, whether in private or in the form of an appreciative statement in front of a group. Recognition primarily relates to good performance or special commitment. The focus here is on the benefit for the company and therefore for all employees. If a positive statement is made in front of a group, the reference to this benefit is always a good addition to promote a sense of community.

When it comes to self-reflection and goal setting, both can also affect non-diverse employees, particularly with regard to the inclusion of diverse employees. The same opportunities for discussion are available here. Non-diverse people also need the opportunity to reflect on themselves, especially when it comes to their relationship with diverse employees.

Such discussions should not have a legal character, but should always aim to ensure that employees recognize their resources in order to realize and actively support Hyper Leadership in the company.

In principle, all employees should have a point of contact that they can use to discuss personal challenges related to Hyper Leadership in the workplace without fear of repercussions. Such a confidential discussion is about recognizing that diverse or non-diverse people do not have "right" or "wrong" personal components, but different ones. The first goal is to accept being different. The second is to learn to appreciate it.

The self-reflection of the various talents often reveals that they have to learn to accept their own differences. Once they have succeeded in doing so, they can perceive themselves as a valuable member of the company and make the best possible use of their resources.

Literature

Diversity Charter 2023, Vielfalt und Diversity - eine Frage der Sichtweise, accessed 28.05.2024, https://www.bochum.de/Charta-der-Vielfalt/Vielfalt-und-Diversity---eine-Frage-der-Sichtweise

Agentur Junges Herz 2021, MEASURES FOR DIVERSITY: HOW COMPANIES CAN PROMOTE DIVERSITY, accessed 28.05.2024, https://www.agentur-jungesherz.de/blog/massnahmen-fuer-diversity-wie-unternehmen-diversity-foerdern-koennen/

Spektrum 2000, Trust, Essay, Christoph Clases and Theo Wehner2000, retrieved 28.05.2024, https://www.spektrum.de/lexikon/psychologie/vertrauen/16374

Missionsustainable 2021, Corporate Culture & Diversity - How important are shared values? Retrieved 28.05.2024, https://missionsustainable.de/2021/02/26/unternehmenskultur-diversity-wie-wichtig-sind-eigentlich-geteilte-werte/

CSR Directive 2023, CSR Directive, accessed 28.05.2024, https://www.umweltbundesamt.de/umweltberichterstattung-csr-richtlinie

Future factor diversity 2023, From vision to everyday life, retrieved 28.05.2024, https://www.charta-der-vielfalt.de/fileadmin/user_upload/Studien_Publikationen_Charta/Charta_der_Vielfalt_-_KMU-Brosch%C3%BCre_2020.pdf

Diversity and inclusion 2023, Diversity and inclusion in recruitment: why you should pay attention, accessed 28.05.2024, https://www.surveymonkey.de/mp/diversity-recruiting/

Future factor diversity 2023, From vision to everyday life, retrieved 28.05.2024, https://www.charta-der-vielfalt.de/fileadmin/user_upload/Studien_Publikationen_Charta/Charta_der_Vielfalt_-_KMU-Brosch%C3%BCre_2020.pdf

Bmfsfj 2023, Sechste Jährliche Information der Bundesregierung über die Entwicklung des Frauenanteils an Führungsebenen und in Gremien der Privatwirtschaft und des öffentlichen Dienstes, retrieved 28.05.2024, https://www.bmfsfj.de/resource/blob/209010/a6daaf83b8e8111e495f5055192ff3c8/bericht-sechste-jaehrliche-information-data.pdf

International Women's Day 2022, International Women's Day: Women's quota in management positions is 24.1 percent, accessed 28.05.2024, https://www.crif.de/pr-events/pressemitteilungen/2022/march/07/weltfrauentag-frauenquote-in-fuehrungspositionen-liegt-bei-24-1-prozent/

Mentoring (2021), What is the difference between mentoring and coaching? Retrieved 28.05.2024, https://www.jobteaser.com/de/advices/was-ist-der-unterschied-zwischen-mentoring-und-coaching

Future factor diversity 2023, From vision to everyday life, accessed 28.05.2024, https://www.charta-der-vielfalt.de/fileadmin/user_upload/Studien_Publikationen_Charta/Charta_der_Vielfalt_-_KMU-Brosch%C3%BCre_2020.pdf

Diversity Coaching 2023, Strengths-oriented to success! Retrieved 28.05.2024, https://business-elf.de/diversity-coaching/

Mentoring (2021), What is the difference between mentoring and coaching? Retrieved 28.05.2024, https://www.jobteaser.com/de/advices/was-ist-der-unterschied-zwischen-mentoring-und-coaching

Adult education 2013, Diversity competence, accessed 28.05.2024, https://erwachsenenbildung.at/themen/diversitymanagement/grundlagen/divkompetenz.php.

6 Development of talents

In order to optimally support diverse people, HR development must use various tools, including the identification of individual dispositions in relation to operational and personal components. Intercultural competence must be promoted at all hierarchical levels. The company environment should implement equal opportunities. Communication channels such as networks should be supported.

6.1 Individual development plans

6.1.1 Determination of requirements and identification of development areas

Company management should monitor the development of employees at least by means of personnel development meetings. This reveals the individual's current status, which may result in a need for further training. If these are carried out regularly, it is possible to fall back on target agreements that have already been set.

It goes without saying that measures are defined in agreement with the employee. Such qualification measures always express appreciation. They are not intended to compensate for deficits, but to promote potential. This is a particularly important aspect when dealing with diverse employees. Development meetings always include a self-assessment as well as an external assessment. If it turns out that diverse talents underestimate their potential, they can be strengthened through appropriate measures (coaching, courses, etc.). Various people tend to underestimate themselves.

At the same time, a person or a working group can be assigned the topic of qualifications so that the further development of specialist knowledge and skills is continuously monitored. By establishing such a task area, a special focus is placed on the specific skills of each person. This is a good basis for promoting various talents.

Qualifications are generally indispensable for career development. For diverse talents, the question arises as to what extent diversity will be incorporated into the new position. This question must be clarified individually, but should be addressed in any case. Hyper Leadership may not play a significant role or it may play a major role. In any case, the importance of Hyper Leadership in a promotion should be discussed with the person so that they have a clear starting position. If, for example, a wheelchair user is being promoted, it may be that the disability has nothing to do with it. However, if a clientele is to be served or expanded in which people with disabilities play a role, it is an important factor.

The further development of employees must be aligned with the future prospects of the company. This can apply to an existing position as well as to a transfer or promotion. Based on the results of the personnel development interviews and also on the findings of Hyper Leadership officers and in cooperation with officers for qualification measures, a suitable person should now be sought. It is important to consider whether there are diverse talents who are suitable. In particular, the aspect of whether and to what extent special Hyper Leadership has already been taken into account for the relevant department must be included. The same criteria must be observed here as in the recruitment process.

Looking at the future prospects of companies in general, it is clear that requirements will change in the coming years, primarily due to digitalization. More than 75% of companies will need more competent employees for this, and more than half will have to establish new fields of activity. However, less than 40% are concerned with determining their qualification requirements in this regard. In addition to problem-solving skills and initiative, the skills in demand include resilience, creativity and intercultural communication (Kofa 2023).

From this point of view, companies that incorporate Hyper Leadership are likely to be in tune with the times and well positioned with their diverse employees. This is because diverse companies are better than average at finding solutions through creative approaches. In addition, diverse talents often prove to be resilient once they are well included.

Intercultural communication speaks for itself. Anyone who employs diverse staff usually already has sufficient points of contact and experience in this area. However, HR management must pay attention to which cultural groups and ethnicities are already represented and whether it should develop further ones for the company. It goes without saying that training is therefore not unnecessary. When people from other cultural backgrounds develop their communication skills, both the management and the employees are well served. The company is well placed to assert itself in the relevant markets.

The skills required for intercultural communication concern a good knowledge of German and other languages. However, the focus is on mediating between different cultures on several levels. In addition to language skills, this also includes knowing how to communicate. While German (and generally Western) speakers tend to be direct, people in Japan and Vietnam, for example, express themselves indirectly. There are big differences between what is considered polite behavior. For example, a business card is handed over with one hand in this country, whereas in East Asia it is always handed over with both hands. Intercultural communication is a broad field for qualification measures, even for the various talents themselves.

6.1.2 Objectives and measurability of development

The overarching objective of a company that promotes Hyper Leadership is to develop and enhance inclusion and Hyper Leadership. Hyper Leadership represents a mix of employees with regard to special, often unique attributes. Inclusion means that differences are not only included as a matter of course, but are also valued. This applies to both diverse and non-diverse employees. The focus is on diverse employees as long as it has not yet been possible to view their Hyper Leadership as a single attribute, just as non-diverse employees also have various individual attributes. Since social development does not correspond to this stage, diverse talents still need special support if they so wish.

In order to achieve this objective as reliably as possible, a company can make a voluntary commitment. It contains a Hyper Leadership strategy in which the individual work areas determine what contribution they can make to achieving this.

Goals can be, for example:

- In the coming x years (the period should be manageable) to increase a number, namely
- older/disabled/female (or other criteria) employees or employees from a different cultural background
- and increase it by x percent (the target should be achievable),
- in connection with new appointments, participation in further training measures, training measures or similar (Kofa 2023).

The introduction of Hyper Leadership management and the development of diverse talent requires not only a strategy, but also a certain amount of time. This development phase is a learning process for everyone involved. Goals that the company has set itself must be evaluated.

Data is required to record and implement this. Of course, HR management can keep track of where certain employees are deployed; the ratio of diverse people to non-diverse people and what Hyper Leadership is involved in each case and, based on this, which diverse talents need to be taken into account when recruiting or implementing.

Factors that affect positive development in relation to Hyper Leadership are sometimes easy to measure, but sometimes only indirectly. In any case, they should be monitored and evaluated. Positive developments can be seen in the following indicators, among others (Kofa 2023).

- The number of vacancies for skilled workers has fallen. The number of vacancies that have been filled has increased. The time from a job advertisement to a vacancy being filled has decreased. This means that the overall fluctuation of employees has fallen.
- The number of applications has risen, particularly because applications from diverse people or from previously underrepresented groups have increased. The number of diverse talents who have risen within the company is in good proportion to the rise of non-diverse talents.
- The company successfully communicates the topic of Hyper Leadership to the outside world. For example, various employees are represented on the website and in newsletters. The company has succeeded in positioning itself as inclusive in the public eye.

- Internally, the topic of Hyper Leadership has a positive connotation. Employees appreciate the inclusive staffing and the good working atmosphere. The number of suggestions and contributions to problem-solving from employees has increased. Employees see innovation and creativity as important contributions to operational development. They have recognized and appreciate that both factors are related to Hyper Leadership. (Employee surveys can be carried out to create measurability).

- Due to the Hyper Leadership, new customer groups could be developed. There may be new business contacts abroad. Customers give positive feedback (surveys can be used for measurability). Perhaps the company has already received recognition or an award for Hyper Leadership.

- Key figures show that turnover and profit have developed positively. Operational processes have been advanced, for example through simplification, systematization, the addition of an important aspect or digitalization. It can be stated that Hyper Leadership played a role in this overall development.

- Targeted further training measures have been implemented, have shown success and are being consistently continued (implementation and planning can be measured). Hyper Leadership management works because there is a contact point specifically for this topic (anonymous evaluations can be carried out, e.g. on the frequency and the topics discussed).

- The working atmosphere has improved and conflicts have been reduced.

- If there is a quality management system, then it regularly shows the process quality, the work quality and thus the product and service quality. There should be a positive development here due to Hyper Leadership.

6.1.3 Training and education

Individual training plans are recommended in order to provide employees with good support. As far as Hyper Leadership is concerned, both diverse and non-diverse people should be trained. The aim is always to create a working atmosphere in which diverse talents are natural members of the company and their special skills and knowledge are integrated, utilized and valued. Of course, non-diverse employees also have their own special skills, which are treated in the same way.

Further training on Hyper Leadership focuses on where the goals of establishing a corresponding corporate culture have not yet been achieved. They are therefore particularly important when building a diverse company. The possibilities of mentoring and coaching, which are also helpful, have already been discussed.

For successful Hyper Leadership management, we recommend training sessions that bring together both diverse and non-diverse people. Here, people can experience and learn how people with different attributes routinely work together. Such measures should be individually tailored.

Communication is always an important factor in this type of training. Everyone involved should learn or improve their ability to speak respectfully to others, taking into account the specific circumstances of each person. Different people have different ideas of politeness. It is often about balancing closeness and distance. In an operational context, it is important that communication is coherent so that professional qualifications can be fully utilized.

There are many points into which Hyper Leadership can be subdivided and which can be dealt with in training and further education measures. Examples include

- What do equal treatment and inclusion mean in practice?
- What advantages does Hyper Leadership bring to the company?
- How does it feel to belong to a generally dominant or diverse social group?
- How can you deal with different attributes in a meaningful way?
- Where are there overlaps and similarities?
- What can good collaboration between diverse and non-diverse employees look like?

- How can respectful communication be ensured and the potential for conflict reduced? (Kofa 2023)

Of course, various talents can also receive individual training and further education. Due to the importance of communication, support in the use of the German language is of great importance. This does not only have to mean language acquisition in the sense of vocabulary and grammar; it can also concern communication strategies, for example with regard to conversations within a customer base or strengthening communicative strategies when personal Hyper Leadership is discussed. There are many external offers in this range of topics, e.g. seminars or courses.

Developing specialist knowledge and skills is possible both externally and internally, and for all employees. Diverse people are no exception here.

On-the-job training is a good way for diverse talents to acquire the skills and knowledge required by their individual workplace, where knowledge transfer and induction take place directly. It is used by many companies for entry-level employees and junior managers. It is valuable for various people because their induction training is completely tailored to them. For example, they can ask any kind of question without feeling uncomfortable. Their induction often results in completely different questions than those of non-diverse people.

For this phase of onboarding (initial period), the company should choose suitably experienced and empathetic members. Then a diverse person can feel secure in this process. Their attributes either play no role or are treated as a matter of course. The person who introduces and accompanies the trainee increasingly takes a back seat, gives feedback and finally lets the trainee work independently. This allows the trainees to systematically develop their task and gradually take on more responsibility (personio 2023).

Further training measures that are often used are taking on additional tasks, e.g. in preparation for a promotion, and job rotation. The latter involves employees changing their job and the associated tasks for a certain period of time (agentur-jungesherz 2021). This measure can be used in a targeted manner to promote various talents. This allows them to get to know a different area of responsibility and thus gain more security. For example, someone can do field work for a while. This procedure is highly recommended before a planned implementation.

Rotation is different from a cross-over, which involves two employees swapping jobs.

"Self-organized learning" is becoming more and more popular. Learners are taking on a great deal of personal responsibility in terms of content and system. The motto is that employees should learn on the job (Blink 2020). With regard to the advancement of digital requirements, it can be assumed that companies will increasingly turn to this form of further training.

Various people should consider whether this method is advisable. In particular, they should not be left alone to continue learning. But it can also be the right choice in some situations or for specific topics. This should be determined together with the various talents.

6.2 Promoting Hyper Leadership in personnel development

6.2.1 Consideration of individual backgrounds and needs

HR management must always keep an eye on what current and future vacancies look like or should look like. Further development does not just mean climbing the career ladder. Implementation can also lead to successful further development, both for the personal skills development of employees and for the effectiveness and turnover of the company. Helpful tools for keeping an overview of everything are

- Regular discussions with employees (e.g. personnel development meetings),
- up-to-date job profiles (job descriptions should be regularly evaluated accordingly),
- a medium and long-term strategy of the company with regard to its organization.

This planning includes considering who is eligible for redeployment or promotion. It is important to keep a close eye on the various employees. In principle, the more transparent and appreciative the corporate culture is, the more attributes recede into the background. Ideally, each individual talent is optimally integrated into the company. This is usually reflected in the success of the company. Nevertheless, no one can rest on their laurels. Companies with a strong commitment to Hyper Leadership in particular should consciously shape personnel development. The following factors should always be kept in mind in the Human Resources department, but they can also be managed well (Diversity Charter 2023).

One group that is often forgotten when it comes to diversity is people whose social background is marked by a rather low level of education. This usually goes hand in hand with relatively little wealth and hardly any access to socially elevated or powerful positions. Members of this group often have to make do with a job in which they cannot develop their skills. It is therefore a good idea to support them from the outset. They often come from non-academic families.

It is possible to pay attention to the social background of trainees and to check where good aptitudes can be recognized. They can then be taken on as trainees. They can be encouraged within the company by involving them in special projects and working groups.

The management level can maintain contact with social institutions or companies that employ people from different social backgrounds and take advantage of opportunities for cooperation. The expansion of networks from this point of view is also helpful.

In an age of demographic change, the age of employees is playing an increasingly important role. It is important to strike a balance between those who are good at developing innovative approaches, especially in the digital field, and those who can draw on a great deal of practical experience. This is why cross-generational measures are often promising. However, there are different attitudes and values. It is important to ensure a respectful atmosphere here. It is particularly helpful if both younger and older employees experience that the other group is helpful. Mentoring programs can also be used for this purpose.

Another aspect that is a hot topic of social discussion (2023) is the equal treatment of all people in terms of gender identity. Gender still often determines how responsibility and resources are distributed within a company. However, the criteria should be skills and expertise. If a certain gender occupies most of the good positions and is the focus of attention much more often than others, there is a tendency, especially on an unconscious level, to favor this gender in other areas and to exclude the others. The danger of unconscious bias must be considered. For this reason, tasks should not be assigned on the basis of gender and groups should be mixed-gender.

There is still no satisfactory general definition of gender itself. Many people describe themselves as transgender, intergender or non-binary. The self-definition of the person concerned must be adopted here.

It is important to use gender in communication, both internally and externally. A company that uses the generic masculine in its public relations work is not credible in terms of Hyper Leadership.

When it comes to pay, equal pay for equal work should be a matter of course.

On a social level, it should be ensured that men can also take parental leave or work part-time without losing prestige or suffering other disadvantages in their job. Same-sex parents should also be able to take parental leave.

Consideration of individual needs is also important when employing people with disabilities. These can be physical, psychological and mental disabilities, but also learning disabilities. People who exhibit physical, cognitive or behavioral characteristics that differ from the usual, unreflected expectations are quickly underestimated and also quickly excluded. This is where cooperation with vocational training centers and the employment agency can help during the recruitment process.

An equal opportunities officer usually takes care of the contacts. HR management should always check whether jobs are suitable for disabled employees. It is important to adapt the jobs to the employees and not the other way around. Accessibility must be guaranteed in all cases. This applies to both mobility and speech. Wheelchair users and people with walking disabilities should be able to reach all stations in the company without any problems (which is also customer-friendly in any case), and workplace instructions and the most important documents should also be available in plain language.

6.2.2 Development of intercultural competence

Intercultural competence is one of the most important skills that must be applied, cultivated and developed in a company with diverse employees. It is not only a matter of course from an ethical point of view to accept people with different cultural or ethnic roots and to work with them on an equal footing; it is also a business necessity to realize inclusion on an intercultural level in view of the shortage of skilled workers.

Intercultural competence is made up of several components. The most important are (Crossculture-academiy 2023):

- On the affective level, tolerance, sensitivity and empathy are necessary.
- On a cognitive level, knowledge of the language, the country and the local culture is important.
- On a communicative level, you need appropriate skills that also include conflict management strategies.

The key qualifications for acquiring cultural competence include openness to the world, flexibility and a willingness to learn. Adaptability and the ability to change perspectives are also required. All components and qualifications can overlap.

In principle, cultural identity is not just created by being born in a certain country. Additionally, it is shaped by several factors such as upbringing, education, age, gender, experiences in working life, political views and sexual orientation. In this respect, intercultural recognition always includes acceptance of the individual.

In the workplace, intercultural competence means understanding the actions and expressions of employees from other cultures and being able to communicate and work with them appropriately. This ability is often also required when interacting in the wider business environment, from customers to suppliers.

One aspect where different cultural norms are noticeable is in greeting rituals. While people in European countries like to shake hands, in Japan and China people introduce themselves with a bow. However, there is also a difference here. The bow is much deeper in Japan. In both cultures, the highest-ranking person is the first to be greeted. If business cards are handed over, this is done with both hands, as this is considered a sign of respect. Direct eye contact tends to be avoided.

In the USA, people shake hands briefly and use a phrase ("How are you?"). A real answer is not expected, rather a "Good, thanks, and you?" is sufficient. In Arab countries, it is customary for men to shake hands with men, but not with women. Women only shake hands with women (Arab rules of conduct 2023).

There are further differences when it comes to the question of how to behave when eating. What is eaten? What topics are allowed to be discussed over a meal? When is small talk required (Crossculture-academy 2023)?

Of course, there are also different cultural ideas within Europe. For people from southern Europe, for example, it is natural not to start the agenda immediately at a meeting, but to first exchange a few personal words and engage in a little small talk. This often does not conform to the German idea of punctuality.

Clothing is also a question of culture. In a business context, good to high-quality clothing is generally considered appropriate. However, the question of what is appropriate can be interpreted differently depending on the culture.

According to a study, the following categories can be used to categorize the different cultural approaches to values (psychologie.springer 2018):

- In the context of etiquette, there are various standards, rules and norms for dealing with uncertain or unclear situations. In practice, for example, a meeting can be a new and therefore unknown situation.
- There are different levels of acceptance for existing power structures and positions and correspondingly different levels of resistance.
- Attitudes towards collectives vary greatly from culture to culture. This affects soft skills such as a sense of duty and loyalty to society, the family and the company.
- The definition of who belongs to the family also varies.
- Whether the sexes have equal rights varies culturally and ethnically.
- Different societies have different desires and ways of dealing with future strategies and perspectives.
- Different moral demands are placed on members of cultural and ethnic communities. This is about values such as fairness and humanity.
- There are different ways of dealing with performance thinking. Achievement is not desired in all social groups and is not always rewarded. This is also related to the extent to which problem-solving thinking is encouraged. The attitude to this in turn results in the attitude

to the question of whether innovations are socially desirable or whether there are efforts to prevent them.

Various possible behaviors within a collective lead to questions. Which actions are considered appropriate? For example, to what extent and by whom is dominant behavior accepted or even valued as a means of assertion?

Developing intercultural competence means at least knowing that such differences exist. Establishing them in the company means being able to understand and classify the behavior of individuals from these backgrounds.

It must be ensured that basic democratic rules apply to all employees - whether they are diverse talents or not. Equal rights and equal treatment are non-negotiable values.

6.2.3 Building networks and exchange opportunities

The use of networks was already an issue in the recruitment process. They are also an important point in personnel development if diverse talents are to be supported and promoted.

A network consists of a limited number of participants who maintain relationships with each other. Networking itself works by first building and then maintaining a network. A network tends to expand, as each contact can generate new contacts (agile-sales 2019).

Companies should facilitate internal networks for their employees. This can be done from a wide variety of perspectives, from part-time employees to expectant mothers or fathers on parental leave to people with a migration background. Of course, Hyper Leadership is not a prerequisite for a network. All employees are equally welcome. However, HR management maintains an overview and naturally has insight at all times. It is a good idea to initiate networks that appeal to diverse talents. The individual networks are initiated together with the HR department. This conveys to employees that management values commitment - including to Hyper Leadership.

The aim of a network is to exchange ideas and support each other. It is therefore well suited for people with the same attributes (e.g. a country of origin or sexual orientation) or in comparable situations (e.g. mothers or fathers). They have comparable experiences and challenges from a certain point of view and can report on their individual solution strategies and successes. Such social networks are intended to improve the working atmosphere and bring employees closer together.

Networks often lead to employees getting to know each other better across hierarchical levels. Ideally, networks are created in which diverse people with different attributes come together. In this way, a corporate culture also develops further in the sense that the company welcomes learning processes based on communication and understanding.

A network can also involve hobbies and leisure activities. One option is sport, another is cooking. This gives employees the opportunity to get to know each other in an informal setting, which promotes the acceptance of Hyper Leadership. In a non-professional context, certain skills can be clearly demonstrated that are then more likely to be seen, demanded and valued in a professional context.

In principle, many diverse people use external networks to help them. A company can support them by informing them internally, for example. This can range from a notice on the notice board to a more detailed presentation in the internal newsletter on all communication channels.

Participation in networks is generally voluntary. Anyone who participates in one should be sure that their contributions are valued. It is therefore a good idea to have a contact person for each internal network group who ensures openness, good manners and an atmosphere of trust. Ideally, this person should be the same as the person who helps to set up the network. Agreements with HR management prior to implementation are therefore important. An adequate framework for networks is crucial if they are to become a constructive innovation factor.

The company can also set up external networks. This is a good opportunity for small and medium-sized enterprises to join forces, for example to plan and implement training measures. Synergy effects can be generated here, particularly with regard to the promotion of diverse employees, for example with joint events such as workshops (Kofa 2023).

Building a network is one of the long-term projects when promoting Hyper Leadership. At the same time, it is in the nature of this communication channel that there is a tendency to expand. The more people participate, the more understanding there is among employees.

In addition to networking, it is good to provide non-digital, direct exchange opportunities. Of course, management must consider how working hours can be reconciled with this. If there are flexible working hours, employees can also meet after work. An attractive location would be ideal. Even aligned canteen opening hours can help. It is also conceivable to set aside time at meetings to discuss Hyper Leadership issues.

It is best to encourage the contact persons of the internal network groups to arrange a physical meeting from time to time. If the topics are suitable, the company can make premises available for this.

6.3 Inclusion in talent development

6.3.1 Breaking down barriers and creating equal opportunities

In practice, equal opportunities often means breaking down barriers. This needs to be done both literally and figuratively. There should be no physical barriers for people with physical disabilities. This is often not easy to achieve. Wheelchair users in particular need barrier-free access to the main entrance and to all floors, which requires an elevator. They also need adequate toilet facilities. Retrofitting here can be costly. It is therefore beneficial for companies that value Hyper Leadership to set up in locations that meet these requirements from the outset.

Desks, desk chairs and aids should be available in the offices for people with severe disabilities to work at and with. The employment agency provides financial support for training and further education as well as the employment of people with disabilities in order to promote equal opportunities. It is worth obtaining information from the relevant local authority (Employment Agency 2023).

A non-physical barrier is a lack of linguistic understanding. Although non-verbal communication plays a large part in overall understanding, language itself is the main medium through which people communicate. A company should always bear in mind that linguistic misunderstandings should be avoided as far as possible and that communicative participation of everyone in internal processes should be ensured. This can mean a longer development. In this case, it should be included as a medium or long-term goal in the catalog of measures for Hyper Leadership.

Training and further education measures are often required to promote language skills. However, it is also worth considering whether to introduce English as the company language, especially if all employees have a basic knowledge of the language. This language can then be systematically trained. At the same time, diverse people who speak a different mother tongue are not disadvantaged. This creates equal language opportunities.

At present (2023), the social discourse is that there are 7.5 million people in Germany who cannot read and write or can only do so inadequately (die-bonn 2023). They are therefore mainly employed as unskilled workers. However, illiteracy as a phenomenon alone says nothing about learning ability. Companies are called upon to consider the extent to which they can contribute to literacy. If employment is not possible, it may be possible to participate in social measures.

Language barriers are also often more subtle (Personalwirtschaft 2023). This can also affect non-diverse people who are more introverted or less self-confident. If these characteristics coincide with Hyper Leadership, special emphasis must be placed on breaking down communicative barriers. Dominant, exclusionary language characterized by hierarchy stands in the way of Hyper Leadership. People who lead groups in particular should constantly reflect on their language and adapt it if necessary. Respectful and appropriate language promotes empathetic cooperation within the team.

One example is gender-inclusive language. In addition to the generic masculine, which requires a certain amount of attention and practice to avoid, there are numerous misogynistic idioms and proverbs that are anchored in common usage. Reflection is always necessary to avoid the pitfalls of a language that has been shaped by masculinity for centuries. Sentences such as "In some countries, people exclude their women" quickly arise, whereas it should be "In some countries, men exclude women". However, a good error culture enables learning processes to take place in the linguistic field.

Internal communication should ensure maximum transparency. Ideally, employees should therefore be kept up to date on all measures and even the small steps that develop Hyper Leadership in the company. One example is notices on the website when there is an innovation in terms of Hyper Leadership. Anything that employees can contribute to inclusion, even at a low-threshold level, is a good reason to communicate it.

Discussion groups also ensure equal opportunities. Depending on how many diverse talents belong to the company, two settings of discussion groups can be maintained. Firstly, one in which representatives of all diverse attributes come together, and secondly, one that is offered to representatives of a single diverse element. Careful consideration needs to be given to who takes the lead in each case. External expert guidance in the form of a coach is often a good choice so that employees have the courage to express their individual needs in a confidential atmosphere. Fundamental results should be communicated with HR management.

The magazine Capital also looked at equal opportunities. One barrier that also prevents equal opportunities is still rigid working hours. Hyper Leadership in companies is not compatible with a culture in which the focus is on who works the longest and hardest. Rather, clear goals and results should be the criteria for success. Creativity and productivity are not promoted by the fact that they must always be achieved within the same amount of time. Nor does value creation automatically increase with the number of hours worked. The option of working from home also enables many employees, including working mothers, to make the most of their performance. Meetings no longer have to be attended physically. A shared channel is sufficient to pass on information. Documenting all important decisions digitally should be a basic principle. This keeps all employees up to date (Capital 2021).

In addition to flexible working hours, offering part-time work is a Hyper Leadership-promoting measure. Part-time work is not only a good way for parents to combine their private life with their job. Many diverse people would like to continue their education in their private lives and need time to do so.

A company should also grant sabbaticals. They enable both continuous further training and longer trips. Both are beneficial to various people. Some stays abroad are only worthwhile after a few weeks.

In order to organize working hours flexibly, HR management needs a good overview of the composition of the teams and the job profiles at all times, as well as opportunities to have a say in the organizational structures.

6.3.2 Creating a supportive environment for individual development

In order to successfully include diverse talents in a company, they should feel valued. An open and supportive environment contributes to this. Each individual should feel that they can contribute their skills and personality.

Especially when building Hyper Leadership structures, it is necessary to explicitly welcome diverse people. This means that clear guidelines against discrimination and harassment in the workplace should be formulated (Shiftbase 2023). They should be made transparent both internally and externally. The company's commitment to Hyper Leadership should not only be known to business partners and customers, but also to suppliers, associations, clubs and other relevant institutions at local and regional level. This creates a safe environment for diverse talents.

Referring to legal texts is the minimum, but not sufficient for credibility. The company should express its commitment in clear terms. This creates an elementary basis of trust for various employees. That way, no one has to fear inappropriate images or unpleasant jokes, for example.

A good working environment is safe, satisfying and supportive. Studies show that three things are particularly important to employees, namely (Experteer 2023)

1. an **interesting job**,
2. **recognition for their work** and
3. **information on the most important matters** and events affecting the company.

The entire working environment contributes to employee satisfaction. This applies to the workplace itself and its facilities, the composition of the team, the working atmosphere and the corporate culture. Regular feedback is also important.

In addition to ergonomic office furniture, smaller things such as a lamp that is bright enough or a fan for hot days can also play a major role in the immediate working environment. You should always actively ask what various employees want, as this can be completely different for each individual.

In terms of communication, it creates a supportive environment if employees are often called by name. Managers should be able to address as many employees as possible personally anyway, even across hierarchical levels.

Rituals create security and trust. This also applies to operational processes. Even small rituals help to create a supportive environment. Team leaders can motivate people to have lunch together, e.g. once a month. Regularity in the sense of a jour fix helps to build trust. There is also nothing wrong with taking a break together for a few minutes to stretch your legs outside or walk around the building. These are small interruptions that do not detract from productivity but develop and strengthen the feeling of togetherness. It is precisely the certainty of belonging that makes a significant contribution to ensuring that all employees can develop individually and develop their talents. In addition, such small breaks from routine work often promote creativity and motivation, and mutual trust is strengthened. Anyone who has to fear envy and resentment will inevitably be hindered in their development. Those who are ostracized or even bullied often have to suppress their skills.

After-work get-togethers strengthen the sense of community and thus create a supportive environment for individual employees. Many people love games. From a visit to the bowling alley to a games evening, there are many possibilities. It is always a good idea for senior employees to get involved. This promotes the confidence that they can be approached. Such experiences are quickly transferred to professional situations.

One of the strongest driving forces in everyday working life is motivation. That's why feedback is so important. Diverse employees in particular should always be motivated by positive feedback. Personal appreciation increases motivation. It is often small things that express recognition, such as congratulations on a birthday. A supportive environment can be promoted by simple means by considering motivating feel-good factors.

According to a survey (Barmer 2022), these include:

- free drinks from the employer,
- a good level of teamwork,
- plants in the offices,
- good coffee,
- appealing interior design and
- small gifts.

The importance of these seemingly minor details is often underestimated by companies. For employees, their job is an important part of their life and they spend many hours at work. They identify with their work and seek fulfillment in it. This is why a positive working environment is very important to them.

Other factors for a good working environment were as follows:

- good working relationship with colleagues and superiors,
- flexible working hours,
- good contact with employees even after work and
- health promotion.

All of these factors can also be implemented in terms of Hyper Leadership. Various employees may prefer good tea to coffee, they may prefer certain plants, or they may have specific, possibly culturally influenced ideas about after-work meetings. Such things are not difficult to take into account and can make a big difference.

Some companies, including many Christian ones, have set up a quiet room where you can retreat for a short period of time. If you follow this example, you can set it up in such a way that it is independent of religion.

6.3.3 Promoting self-confidence and self-reflection

Self-confidence is an essential quality to be able to withstand the demands of the world of work. This is particularly true for diverse people who, in addition to the routine physical, mental and cognitive demands, must also be stable in terms of their Hyper Leadership. The American dictionary "Merriam webster" provides a differentiated definition of self-confidence (merriam-webster 2023). According to this, it is "a feeling or awareness of one's own strength as well as confidence in one's own abilities".

This shows that both emotional and cognitive factors play a role. Self-confidence can remain as a feeling in the preconscious or exist as a clear idea in the consciousness of an individual. Employers should endeavor to facilitate or support the process from mere feeling to awareness of self-confidence for various employees. The same applies to confidence in one's own abilities.

Self-confidence includes authenticity. This means accepting your own value system and being able to defend it in case of doubt. At the same time, self-confidence should not turn into arrogance. It is important to find a healthy balance between assertiveness and modesty (diversityjobgroup 2023). Self-confidence and self-reflection are therefore linked. This poses an additional challenge for diverse talents with regard to their particular attributes.

Decision-making processes are helpful in order to develop appropriate self-confidence, but also to allow for self-reflection. It should always be sufficiently clear to diverse employees that they bear responsibility and make decisions in their area of work. Working conditions and corporate culture contribute to the development of healthy, i.e. adequate, self-confidence. At the same time, self-reflection on decisions made and their effects must be possible. An open error culture is of great importance here.

When mistakes are made, the focus should be on analyzing the circumstances that led to them and developing strategies for avoiding them in the future. Assigning blame would not be good personnel management. Anyone who has made a mistake bears responsibility, but the next step is to focus on the causes and the opportunities for change. Establishing a causal link between mistakes and a diverse attribute would be fatal and the opposite of inclusion. Diverse people should have the certainty that this will not happen. Then a lot has already been done for their self-confidence and their ability to self-reflect. This also promotes their confidence in being able to communicate issues and challenges, whether in their team or to superiors. Diverse talents should always be encouraged to seek out communication on their own initiative.

A good way to strengthen the self-confidence of diverse employees is to actively involve them in measures and projects. If Hyper Leadership is presented as a corporate principle on the website - which should be the case - you can always include different diverse people in the presentations. Presenting only a few and always the same diverse people doing the same activities for months on end would not be good public relations work. Changes are important and create credibility and authenticity.

In addition, various employees should accompany external activities of the company, such as visits to universities. Newsletters can introduce various people or show them working on a specific project. New employees should be introduced within the internal communication channels anyway, and should be given the opportunity to speak for themselves, at least in the form of quotes. Even such supposedly small contributions increase self-confidence.

Of course, self-confidence and self-reflection are also promoted by the many measures that have already been mentioned. These include targeted mentoring and coaching, individually tailored training, motivation to participate in internal networks and discussions in different contexts. Temporary job changes are also part of this. Even the perception or knowledge that non-diverse employees are being trained in Hyper Leadership increases the self-confidence of diverse people.

Telling success stories is part of a company's public relations work. In the best-case scenario, employees and, of course, various people should always set a good example in their portrayals. When marketing and advertising campaigns are running, various talents should be involved.

Of course, it is also necessary for non-diverse employees to have adequate self-confidence. They may also need to strengthen it. As far as self-reflection is concerned, it is also required for non-diverse employees, at least with regard to their attitude towards people with special attributes and their own contribution to promoting and supporting Hyper Leadership in the company. Promoting diverse talents never means neglecting non-diverse talents. Every HR management team must face up to this potential balancing act.

Literature

Kofa 2023, DiversityManagement.pdf, accessed 28.05.2024,
https://www.kofa.de/personalarbeit/unternehmenskultur/diversity-management/

Personio 2023, Training on the job: advantages, methods and requirements, retrieved
28.05.2024, https://www.personio.de/hr-lexikon/training-on-the-job/

agentur-jungesherz 2021, JOB ROTATION - DEFINITION, PROCEDURES
AND PRACTICE, accessed 28.05.2024, https://www.agentur-jungesherz.de/hr-
glossar/job-rotation-definition-vorgehensweise-und-praxis/

Blink 2020, How do you teach employees self-organized learning, accessed
28.05.2024, https://www.blink.it/blog/mitarbeitern-selbstorganisiertes-lernen-
vermitteln

Diversity Charter 2023, What you can do, accessed 28.05.2024, https://www.charta-
der-vielfalt.de/fuer-arbeitgebende/vielfaltsdimensionen/soziale-herkunft/

Crossculture-academiy 2023, Intercultural competence - why at all? (Definition,
examples, models), retrieved 28.05.2024, https://crossculture-
academy.com/interkulturelle-kompetenz/

Arab rules of conduct 2023, Business etiquette for Arab countries, retrieved
28.05.2024, https://www.business-wissen.de/artikel/arabische-verhaltensregeln-
business-knigge-fuer-arabische-laender/

psychologie.springer 2018, Kulturelle Unterschiede und interkulturelle Kompetenz,
accessed 31.10.2023, https://lehrbuch-
psychologie.springer.com/sites/default/files/atoms/files/webexkurs_fichter_kulturelle_un
terschiede_und_interkulturelle_kompetenz.pdf

Agile-sales 2019, NETWORKING IN THE COMPANY 2019, accessed
28.05.2024, https://www.agile-sales-company.de/blog/netzwerken-im-unternehmen

Employment Agency 2023, Promotion of people with disabilities, accessed
28.05.2024, https://www.arbeitsagentur.de/unternehmen/finanziell/foerderung-
menschen-mit-behinderungen

Personalwirtschaft 2023, How must HR communicate to anchor DEI in the
company? Retrieved 28.05.2024, https://www.personalwirtschaft.de/news/hr-
organisation/wie-muss-hr-kommunizieren-um-dei-im-unternehmen-zu-verankern-
156593/

Capital 2021, How companies can ensure more equal opportunities now, retrieved 28.05.2024 https://www.capital.de/karriere/wie-unternehmen-jetzt-fuer-mehr-chancengleichheit-sorgen-koennen

Die-bonn 2023, Literacy, accessed 28.05.2024, https://www.die-bonn.de/doks/2013-alphabetisierung-01.pdf

Barmer 2022, Work motivation: What motivates working people in their job?, accessed 28.05.2024, https://www.barmer.de/firmenkunden/gesund-arbeiten/gesundheit-im-beruf/arbeitsmotivation-1056836

Shiftbase 2023, Diversity in the workplace: Strengthen your company, accessed 28.05.2024, https://www.shiftbase.com/de/blog/diversity-am-arbeitsplatz

Experteer 2023, How to create a satisfied working environment 2023, accessed 28.05.2024, https://www.experteer.de/magazin/management-skills-so-schaffen-sie-ein-zufriedenes-arbeitsumfeld/

merriam-webster 2023, self-confidence, accessed 28.05.2024, https://www.merriam-webster.com/dictionary/self-confidence

diversityjobgroup 2023, Inclusion and trust in the world of work, accessed 28.05.2024, https://.ch/inklusion-und-vertrauen/

7 Practical challenges and solutions

Company awareness-raising measures are essential for the practical implementation of Hyper Leadership. Targeted training for the entire workforce is also required. The management level should always be a role model for Hyper Leadership, even within its own ranks. Conflict management must be included in the catalog of measures, and target agreements and evaluation are essential.

From Theory to Practice:
Implementing Hyper Leadership for Enhanced Organizational Agility

While the theoretical benefits of Hyper Leadership are clear, organizations often struggle with practical implementation. This chapter addresses common challenges and provides actionable solutions for organizations transitioning toward a hyper-agile framework through effective leadership practices.

The Awareness Challenge: Limited Understanding

Many organizations face resistance due to incomplete understanding of Hyper Leadership principles and their connection to agility. Solutions:

1. Structured Awareness Programs
- Regular town halls focusing on diversity and agility success stories
- Monthly newsletters highlighting practical applications
- Case study presentations from different departments
- Visual aids and infographics throughout workplace spaces

2. Experiential Learning
- Role-playing exercises demonstrating diverse scenarios
- Simulation workshops for complex decision-making
- Cross-cultural exchange programs
- Job shadowing across departments

Traditional management skills may not adequately support hyper leadership requirements. Solutions:

1. Comprehensive Training Framework
- Leadership development programs focused on inclusive practices
- Cultural competency workshops
- Emotional intelligence training
- Agile methodology certification programs

2. Targeted Skill Enhancement
- Conflict resolution techniques
- Cross-cultural communication skills
- Change management expertise
- Digital collaboration tools mastery

Management Role Modeling: Inconsistent Leadership Behaviors

Leaders may unconsciously maintain traditional hierarchical approaches. Solutions:

1. Leadership Accountability Measures
- 360-degree feedback mechanisms
- Regular leadership behavior assessments
- Peer review systems
- Performance metrics tied to inclusive leadership practices

2. Visible Leadership Actions
- Regular participation in diverse team activities
- Public commitment to diversity goals
- Transparent decision-making processes
- Active mentorship programs

Conflict Management: Increased Complexity in Diverse Teams

Different perspectives and working styles can lead to more frequent conflicts. Solutions:

1. Preventive Measures
- Early warning systems for potential conflicts
- Cultural sensitivity training
- Clear communication protocols
- Established mediation procedures

2. Resolution Framework
- Dedicated conflict resolution teams
- Multi-step escalation processes
- Cultural mediators
- Regular team-building exercises

Evaluation and Metrics: Measuring Success

Traditional metrics may not capture the full impact of Hyper Leadership initiatives. Solutions:

1. Comprehensive Measurement System
- Diversity metrics dashboard
- Agility response times
- Employee satisfaction indices
- Innovation metrics across diverse teams

2. Regular Assessment Tools
- Quarterly diversity audits
- Team effectiveness surveys
- Leadership behavior assessments
- Return on investment calculations for diversity initiatives

Phase 1: Foundation Building

1. Assessment
   - Current state analysis
   - Gap identification
   - Resource evaluation
   - Stakeholder mapping

2. Planning
   - Timeline development
   - Resource allocation
   - Communication strategy
   - Training schedule

Phase 2: Active Implementation

1. Roll-out
   - Pilot programs
   - Department-specific initiatives
   - Training sessions
   - Communication campaigns

2. Monitoring
   - Progress tracking
   - Feedback collection
   - Adjustment mechanisms
   - Success celebration

Phase 3: Sustainability

1. Integration
   - System alignment
   - Policy updates
   - Process modifications
   - Cultural reinforcement

2. Continuous Improvement
   - Regular reviews
   - Update mechanisms
   - Innovation incorporation
   - Best practice sharing

Best Practices for Success

1. Clear Communication
   - Regular updates
   - Multiple channels
   - Two-way feedback loops
   - Transparent reporting

2. Stakeholder Engagement
   - Employee resource groups
   - Leadership councils
   - Cross-functional teams
   - External partnerships

3. Resource Allocation
   - Dedicated budget
   - Time investment
   - Personnel assignment
   - Technology support

4. Change Management
- Resistance management
- Progress celebration
- Success recognition
- Course correction

Common Pitfalls to Avoid

1. Implementation Errors
- Rushing the process
- Inadequate resources
- Poor communication
- Lack of follow-through

2. Cultural Missteps
- Superficial approaches
- Tokenism
- Cultural insensitivity
- Exclusive practices

The successful implementation of Hyper Leadership requires a systematic approach that addresses practical challenges while maintaining focus on the ultimate goal of organizational agility. By following these structured solutions and maintaining commitment to continuous improvement, organizations can transform theoretical understanding into practical success.

The key to success lies in recognizing that implementing Hyper Leadership is not a destination but a journey of continuous evolution. Organizations must remain flexible and responsive, adjusting their approach based on feedback and results while maintaining unwavering commitment to the principles of inclusive leadership and organizational agility.

7.1 Dealing with prejudices and stereotypes

7.1.1 Raising awareness

Prejudices and stereotypes against various people are based on attitudes that are more or less radically opposed to those who think and act differently. The question here is not whether these people do something that harms others. It is merely a question of whether they deviate from certain ideas of how people should be and how they should behave. That is why it is discrimination. Prejudice does not ask whether, for example, appearance, a religious attitude or (non-)belonging to a gender actually has harmful effects. If they did, they would cancel themselves out, because you quickly realize that such attributions are absurd. Prejudices unjustifiably attribute characteristics to people on the basis of attributes from which nothing can be objectively derived. In most cases, these are negative characteristics.

If there is uncertainty as to whether prejudices exist, a test is helpful. There are several options for this.

A fundamental measure against prejudices and stereotypes is education. In this respect, companies in the western world benefit from the fact that education is highly valued in secular countries.

Biases are often deeply rooted. In order to cultivate Hyper Leadership, it is important to break them down. To this end, HR management can consciously question or make every decision against the background of whether it has anchored such ideas in itself and counteract them accordingly. At the same time, company management should regularly provide information on current - scientific and practical - findings, e.g. with articles in the internal newsletter. It can also involve external speakers. The following topics are still relevant (Synergy-through-diversity 2023).

Women

There is social pressure for women to participate more in working life. However, it is often limited to the generally formulated term "advancement of women" and suggests that women's deficits must be eliminated. However, it is not women who have deficits, but rather deficits in their inclusion in the world of work. In fact, around 46% of women are in employment, but almost three quarters of them work part-time. One example of an image that needs to be counteracted is that a woman typically sits in the front office but not in the boss's chair. The compatibility of career and family, which is often demanded for women, is only one factor that can sometimes even promote stereotypical role distributions between women and men.

The question of what motivates women to better advance their careers should be given greater consideration. Structural factors, e.g. the provision of childcare, but also the breaking of gender-specific thought patterns, are beneficial. For example, women often have qualifications that are neglected in the selection process for promotions. Sometimes this is partly due to the fact that women work part-time.

Age

The second factor that should be addressed is age. From the mid-2020s, it is expected that around 40% of the workforce will be between 30 and 50 years old and a further 40% older. The remaining workforce will be aged 30 and under. It is therefore necessary to break down entrenched ideas. This includes the common belief that only young people are strong, capable and mentally fit. The interaction between younger and older people should be encouraged.

Older employees usually have extensive specialist knowledge and remain confident in stressful situations. Younger and older employees can complement each other well. This has been recognized in the USA. There is a campaign there called "Hire your mom", which calls for older women to be hired because they are reliable, resilient and hard-working (HAZ 2023). Remuneration also needs to be reconsidered. The fact that salary increases are automatically linked to advancing age does not have to be the sole reason for better pay. Performance could also be a criterion here.

Intercultural issue

Intercultural factors are a constant topic of discussion in society. In Germany, 25% of the population had an intercultural background in 2018. This includes both foreign people and those with a migrant background. In addition, there are the descendants of families with a migration background as well as naturalized citizens and ethnic German repatriates.

There are now many companies that prove that a multicultural workforce increases turnover and promotes development processes. However, internal concerns often still need to be dispelled through educational work. Intercultural skills are becoming increasingly necessary due to globalization. More and more international teams are being created (even on a virtual level).

Disabilities

The concept of inclusion now exists at a societal level. It stands for the natural inclusion of all people in social processes. Diversity should be considered normality. However, the word "inclusion" originally paved the way for people with disabilities to enter the public eye. Education is often particularly important for them. A physical impairment must not lead to it being ignored, trivialized or inferred as a deficiency in cognitive abilities. People with disabilities are often particularly motivated to work and perform. People of short stature are still not employed simply because companies are unable to provide them with suitable work equipment.

Other impairments also often lead to prejudice. Examples include dyslexia and dyscalculia. Both represent a weakness in one area but say nothing fundamental about intelligence and performance. In Germany, around 12 percent of the population is affected by one of these two impairments. There are also people with a learning disability. It should also be possible to find a job for them. As a rule, they feel comfortable with constant, manageable activities. The educational work here is that there is no reason to look down on them because of this. Their performance is no less valuable.

It should go without saying that a company that values diversity should meet the statutory minimum quota of 5% people with disabilities in its employment rate.

There are also people who have a special talent - the insular talent. An insular talent is characterized by an excellent memory and often also has special talents or abilities (socialnet 2020). As severely autistic people generally do not meet the usual requirements when it comes to communication, they are often underestimated. For example, their ability to use language in a targeted manner is often limited, which is why it makes sense to use images. Furthermore, they do not respond to the full extent (generally expected) to offers of contact and requests because they are often overwhelmed by the speed and quantity of verbal utterances. They do not understand sarcasm, irony and metaphors. (autistenhilfe 2023). However, their special skills can be an advantage in a company in a specific area.

Sexual orientation

Sexual orientation is the diversity dimension that is least discussed in public. It is still taboo. People who feel socially disadvantaged in this respect need a good working environment, and education about the equal value of people of all sexual orientations is also necessary in companies. These employees should not be forced into a dual role. For example, they should also be allowed to display photos of their loved ones on their desks and report on their relationships and vacations in a relaxed manner. In addition, homosexual employees are often important for companies because homosexual people represent an entire customer group.

At present (2023), the question of which toilet facilities should be offered is a matter of social debate. There is still no clarification and no legal regulation.

Religion and worldview

A company should also provide information on religion and ideology. They are often subsumed under the aspect of culture, but this does not cover all aspects. Religious beliefs in particular can have an impact on other areas, such as social behavior. At the same time, they can be associated with special needs, such as times and spaces for religious rituals.

Religions and world views are a particularly sensitive area. As a rule, they are among the most important resources for motivated action. They should not be seen as a threat, but as a form of knowledge, experience and conviction. This is why it is important to provide information about different directions within the company. In Germany, around 36% of the population do not belong to any religious denomination. A further 29 % of people belong to a Christian church and 4 % to Islam. However, other religions and world views are practiced, including Buddhism.

For companies, it is generally a learning process to see educational work as part of their remit. But it pays off.

7.1.2 Hyper Leadership training

Training courses are events in which a subject is not only explained in general terms, but also in detail. In addition, there is the active participation of the participants. A purely receptive absorption of material does not make educational sense. Acting, in addition to thinking, ensures that the learning effect is maintained. In contrast to educational work, which addresses the cognitive level of employees and can be covered with information, emotional intelligence should always be required in training courses and workshops.

The chambers of industry and commerce, as well as other organizations, offer not only training and workshops, but also materials. Groups with diverse and non-diverse participants are particularly effective.

Training and further education have already been discussed. In addition, a possible process will be presented here using intercultural learning as an example (IKUD Seminars 2023).

1. In the first step, a critical action is presented in which intercultural encounters play a role. The participants observe the process. Then they present their own perceptions and interpretations.
2. This is followed by an exchange on the various interpretations. This brings new perspectives into the discussion. In this way, the situation is viewed

from different angles and the perception of what is presented can be expanded or changed.

3. This is followed by a reflection on the various aspects that led to different interpretations. Various cultural circumstances and their consequences are explicitly discussed. Necessary additions are made. The new findings are presented.

Learning objectives can be, for example: to question an unreflected evaluation process, to reconsider one's own cultural standards and to reflect on and/or change one's own expectations in intercultural situations.

7.2 Creating an inclusive work culture

7.2.1 Managers as role models

In a company that sees leadership as a natural component, it is essential that the management level not only supports the corresponding attitude, but also demands and exemplifies it.

It should therefore be a matter of course that, for example, members of management work part-time, are in wheelchairs, are female or belong to a social minority.

At the same time, a clear stance should be recognizable, both internally and externally. Positioning leadership as a value in itself and the benefits of leadership for the company strengthens the backing of all employees. For example, you can take part in local activities and events organized by organizations or institutions. Examples include alliances for open-mindedness or individual initiatives on fairness, diversity, inclusion and the like. Supporting nationwide campaigns is also conceivable (Diversity Charter 2023).

The company should regularly take part in competitions and forums that focus on inclusion and diversity, e.g. for best practice.

In any case, management should formulate and publicize a commitment to diversity that communicates diversity as a social necessity as well as a benefit for the company. Depending on the company, a moral (or Christian) justification may also be useful. This presentation can be developed together with employees and evaluated at a later date. It is a good idea to specify precise goals and discuss them with the relevant departments. Examples are (Kofa 2023):

The company plans to discontinue:
- persons with disabilities
- trainees with a migration background
- older employees
- other diverse talents

Over the next few years, the company plans to
- introduce more flexible working time models,
- to promote respectful cooperation (e.g. through training and workshops) and
- install a mentoring program.

Milestones and a careful analysis of financial resources and the personnel situation are recommended for such planning. Above all, the time frame and concrete figures should be specified. For example:
- a person with a disability within the next two years
- two trainees with a migration background within the next year
- at least one employee aged 50 or over in the next 18 months

Communication is one of the most important factors. Interdepartmental meetings are a particularly helpful tool for implementing, but also for maintaining and cultivating diversity. Managers should therefore be in regular contact with the individual departments (their management and employees). All employees should be motivated to do their best to achieve the goals (Kofa 2023).

The behavior of the management team should set an example at all times. For open self-reflection, which is also easy to accept, it makes sense to carry out supervision from time to time.

Leadership-related questions are helpful for managers. Examples are

- Do we regularly praise and recognize the performance of various employees?
- Do we actively demand contributions from employees for Leadership?
- Do we ensure a positive working atmosphere that accepts and promotes Leadership?
- Are the relationships between managers and employees characterized by trust?
- Does the management make its decisions transparent, also with regard to Leadership?

The mindset of management always has an impact on the overall working atmosphere. Dealing constructively with mistakes is one aspect that contributes to a good working atmosphere. At the same time, there should be a fundamental openness.

Employees must also be allowed to express their worries and fears. One option for this is an "ideas and concerns box". It can be installed physically as a kind of bulletin board or made available virtually. All employees can address challenges here. Feedback should also be included.

7.2.2 Promotion of exchange and cooperation

For good cooperation and communication, it is important that there is mutual understanding among employees. It is also important that individuals are satisfied. Many topics that affect diverse people should be integrated as a matter of course in operational procedures, guiding documents and checklists. The aim is to make Hyper Leadership a matter of course and to push questioning more and more into the background. Management can do a lot to achieve this (Diversity Charter 2023).

At the HR management level, it is advisable to provide contact persons for employees. If no separate positions can be created for this purpose, it is possible to assign the area of responsibility to suitable employees. This can be a comprehensive spectrum that affects all diverse people. However, it can also be differentiated. For example, there can be equal opportunities officers (with the area of gender equality), disability managers (with the area of disability) or diversity officers (for all diverse people).

A company complaints office can also be set up so that non-diverse employees also have an opportunity for discussion, suggestions and possibly changes. In addition, a generally accessible feedback box can be set up that also takes anonymous contributions seriously. There is no need for a feedback meeting.

Various religious and cultural celebrations must be taken into account when organizing working hours. Employees may need leave on certain days. An intercultural calendar is a good tool for planning. A public diversity calendar that shows international days on which diversity is celebrated is also suitable. Company events can be held on these days (agentur-jungesherz 2021).

People with disabilities need a reserved parking space in front of the building complex. For employees with children or family members in need of care, it is important to have flexible working hours. An on-site childcare facility is ideal. A proportion of employees working from home promotes general satisfaction.

Various people should always be involved in campaigns, from a publicity campaign to working groups to participation in competitions or regional activities. Successes such as awards and prizes, but also participation alone, can showcase public relations work in many places.

Guidelines are suitable for employee communication, for example on gender-appropriate language. Courses on this, as well as on the German language in general, are also available. Cross-departmental and cross-hierarchical discussions on the topic of diversity can take place during or outside of working hours.

Internally, it is important not only to demand the avoidance of prejudices and stereotypes, but also to actively intervene immediately when they occur. Managers in particular must always be up to date. Due to modern media, there are constantly new terms that need to be questioned. Management should have a good command of communication strategies, but also be up to date on content, for example on culturally specific topics.

The canteen is an important place, not only for providing food, but also for meeting people. Different people need different food options, including vegan, vegetarian, kosher, halal and also dishes from other countries or cultures. There can be weeks of "vegetarian, African etc." food.

In principle, good health management is a proven means of promoting a sense of togetherness and team spirit - apart from the fact that it also reduces the sickness rate. The options range from subsidies for health-promoting courses to the company's own sports hall or fitness room.

One good option is the "Lunch & Learn" campaign. This is a learning format that promotes internal training and communication. It can be held regularly, e.g. every two months. Management invites employees to a short event over lunch. Extending the lunch break is helpful. The company can provide the food on this day, or the employees can bring their own. A short presentation provides a brief, precise introduction, followed by a discussion round. Short, clear topics are ideal for this measure. Rooms other than the canteen, such as an event room, are suitable for this activity. As this is a lunchtime activity, participation must be voluntary (akademie 2022).

It should be mentioned once again that job rotation is an excellent way of promoting mutual understanding. Consideration should be given to implementing measures between diverse and non-diverse people in particular. It can be implemented across departments and business units and even at an international level if the business relationships are appropriate.

7.2.3 Conflict resolution strategies for diverse teams

In principle, a company can keep the potential for conflict as low as possible through a good, open working atmosphere as well as through forms of discussion at several levels (which have already been discussed). In the event of conflict, the relevant contact person can also try to resolve it first, e.g. the diversity officer. In principle, mentoring and coaching are an option for individuals who are experiencing conflict with another person. The company can also use anonymous employee surveys to gain an overview of potential conflicts from time to time and intervene in good time. Nevertheless, conflicts cannot always be avoided.

Conflicts often arise from recurring differences of opinion, which often harden the fronts and impair appropriate communication. In such cases, there are two options, namely collegial case counseling as an internal measure and mediation, for which an external certified person should be chosen to lead the process.

Mediation is a proven method for conflict resolution. This applies to private incidents as well as business disputes. It is a confidential and structured procedure. The procedure is suitable for conflicts between employees with equal rights on the one hand and between employees and managers on the other.

The aim is to find an amicable and satisfactory solution for the parties to the conflict through communication. In any case, it must be guaranteed that the mediation is independent and neutral. This is an essential prerequisite (Wirtschaftslexikon 2023). You should therefore engage a person who is certified in mediation (and not settle for someone who only has further training without a certificate). An external specialist is best suited. People who belong to the company could be biased, even if unconsciously.

The person leading the mediation ensures that both parties receive equal understanding. The aim is for the parties to the conflict to at least accept each other's points of view and, ideally, to be able to understand or even comprehend them. In this way, a solution can be found that is at least acceptable and, in the best case, satisfactory for both sides. Mediation should never end with a losing party, but rather create a win-win situation. There is a law for mediation (Mediation Act, BGBI I of 21.07.2012, p. 1577). It stipulates confidentiality.

Due to his/her impartiality, the mediator can mediate between the parties. Participation in the process is fundamentally voluntary. It requires that the parties get involved on a factual and emotional level in order to find a good solution for themselves and the other party.

Intercultural and intergenerational complications are often an issue in the workplace. Different cultures (and religions) often have different feelings of identity. In many cases, this is due to different interpretations of:

- norms and customs
- linguistic conventions
- customs and traditions
- the feeling of time
- the feeling of honor
- the concept of appropriateness in actions

Conflicts between older and younger employees are often about the appreciation of age and life experience as well as respectful treatment. It also plays a role that younger people do not feel sufficiently accepted and seen in their competence (bmev.de 2023).

When managers have differences with subordinates, peer counseling is a recommended tool. This is self-directed coaching that takes place on a voluntary basis. The exchange is focused on a specific problem. A team of four to five people from the same senior hierarchical level is put together, ideally with an interdisciplinary composition, and a moderator, a case-giver and the person or persons providing advice are determined. The time limit should be 60 to 90 minutes.

The person presenting the case presents their problem, for example the difficulty a co-worker is having adapting to their team or taking on a new task. The counselors then present possible solutions and courses of action based on their own experiences. The person presenting the case receives feedback.

In this process, mutual trust and the agreement of confidentiality are fundamental prerequisites. The person presenting the case must be open to new solutions and the counselors must treat them and their problem with respect and empathy. If this is successful, this method offers a cost-effective and timely solution to conflicts. The team members can also reflect on and professionalize their own leadership style. (gotscharek-company 2023)

7.3 Performance management

7.3.1 Target agreements

In order to establish Hyper Leadership in the company fundamentally and in the long term, target agreements for a wide range of areas are a good guide. They should set out the requirements you are facing, the changes this entails and what you want to achieve. The second step is to evaluate what has been achieved in a certain period of time (see next chapter).

The basis of the target agreement is an analysis of the current situation, which is to be transformed into a target situation. It begins with which various people are to be employed in which departments. Transfers should also be considered here. For onboarding (arrival at the company), one objective should be to define and adhere to guidelines or a checklist. This includes welcoming letters to new employees, their introduction by a competent person or team and cross-departmental introductions within the company. The offboarding (departure) of employees should also be managed as far as it is foreseeable. It goes without saying that this should be done in an appreciative manner.

It is a challenge to establish Hyper Leadership as a matter of course in day-to-day operations. A target agreement should be to include Hyper Leadership management in day-to-day business and to give it the necessary importance. This requires good time management.

The inclusion of Hyper Leadership within the various types of meetings is another point for setting objectives. For example, the discussion of Leadership-related experiences can be made mandatory for a personnel development meeting. The right of diverse employees to consult a contact person confidentially is also a target.

Further training and support measures (e.g. training courses, workshops, mentoring and coaching) must always be defined as objectives. As far as possible, people should be assigned to the measures in order to enable scheduling. Employees must also be able to adapt to this. A person who is specifically (exclusively or additionally) tasked with further training and the like is a good source of support.

The working environment should be characterized by an appreciative atmosphere. To this end, appropriate measures can be defined (e.g. rules for the use of language, inclusion of diverse employees in campaigns and working groups, representation of diverse employees in public relations work).

Participation in activities of all kinds relating to leadership is part of the planning of objectives. In Germany, for example, there is the "Leadership Day", in which numerous media participate. The focus here is on reducing discrimination of all kinds and promoting equal opportunities.

An important objective concerns the economic development of the company. If possible, it should expand its product range in terms of leadership. There is already a market for many of these items, so there are opportunities to expand the customer base.

Stakeholders should also be repeatedly encouraged and motivated to support leadership. Stakeholders are all persons, groups and institutions that are directly or indirectly involved in a company's activities. In addition to the customer base, these include trading partners, suppliers, administrative bodies such as public administration, investors, clubs, associations and other organizations, including political ones. Greater value creation is also a goal that fits in with leadership. Other projects relate to giving preference in tenders to suppliers that are committed to leadership.

In terms of communication, the management level can set itself the goal of regularly exchanging experiences with other companies and expanding networks.

It is generally a good idea to operationalize target agreements as much as possible. This involves defining manageable concrete steps within a time period. This makes implementation easier and more manageable. Evaluation takes place at the end of the period.

7.3.2 Reviews

In order to assess whether and to what extent the goals of implementing leadership have been achieved, evaluations must be carried out. Systematic controlling is the best solution for this. Wherever possible, there should be key figures so that measurement can be as objective as possible. A good corporate culture has a whole range of indicators because they provide data on the status quo and where improvements are needed. Examples from HR management are sick leave and length of service in the company.

The following criteria can be used to evaluate the processes (Diversity Charter 2023).

- The idea of Hyper Leadership runs through the entire organization. Leadership shapes the corporate culture and the working atmosphere. It is recognizable in all processes. Leadership management is implemented as a key feature from the lowest level of the hierarchy right up to management. Managers have a special responsibility in this regard.

- HR management regularly reviews where non-diverse, strongly homogeneous structures have formed and finds strategies to dissolve them. Such processes can quickly take on a life of their own, whether due to carelessness in personnel deployment or unconscious motives (such as unconscious bias).

- The aim is to optimally combine employees' skills with the company's performance requirements, taking into account diverse and other special talents.
- Leadership is treated transparently within the company. Detailed information should be provided at least once a year. There are several options for reporting. In addition to the newsletter, intranet and website, strategies and successes can be explained in HR reporting (personnel report). This discloses the key figures based on data collection.
- Annual reports are also suitable for this purpose. Companies also present CSR reports. These provide information on compliance with the Supply Chain Due Diligence Act. It obliges German companies to exercise due diligence that respects human rights (CSR 2023).
- The company uses various methods to create transparency about its commitment to leadership. Externally, this includes press releases and information on the website, for example. Within the company, for example, events are held to provide information about the development of leadership and its great importance.
- The company also values the general social commitment to leadership. The company's actions in the market are geared towards this. The company participates in corresponding campaigns.
- The workforce is involved in the establishment and implementation of leadership. This is aided, among other things, by support in building employee networks. Company interest groups are also established.

Helpful questions for the management are with regard to the internal process:

1. Which people already guarantee the implementation of leadership in the entire organizational structure?
2. What is needed so that diverse employees can develop their full talent and potential?
3. Which conditions are already fulfilled and which still need to be created?
4. What changes are needed to create the right conditions?

The following questions are helpful with regard to the external process:

1. Which target groups are already helpful and which still need to be developed?
2. Is the marketing department aware of all the needs and expectations of the target groups? Which ones still need to be identified?
3. Are there still no employees in the workforce who meet these needs and expectations?
4. Are some of the employees able to use their talents and potential to develop new products and new business relationships?

Careful assessments and evaluations not only serve to establish diverse talents, but also provide a good overview of the overall situation of the company.

7.3.3 Recognition

Recognition and appreciation of employees are key motivators for successfully shaping the work process. This applies to both diverse and non-diverse people. Unfortunately, both are often neglected. While recognition refers to the acknowledgement of performance, appreciation refers to the acceptance of the entire personality.

With regard to Hyper Leadership, recognition should not only be given to various employees, but also to all those who actively support the establishment and implementation of Hyper Leadership. In a mixed team, for example, it would not make sense to recognize only a few members instead of praising the entire team. Nevertheless, diverse people are often more sensitive to recognition or lack of recognition.

There are several international surveys from recent years on the importance of recognition (atlassian 2023). According to these surveys, employee turnover is 31% lower at companies that give recognition than at others. In one study, 21% of employees who did not feel recognized left their current company within a quarter, while only 12% of those who felt recognized did so. 81% of employees stated that they are willing to work harder when they receive recognition. A company culture that fosters recognition is much better received by 46% of job seekers, and 32% look at the company's ratings on this point before applying.

Recognition can manifest itself in various forms. Worthy of praise are not only exceptional results that may have taken a long time to achieve, but also well-done selective results. They occur again and again in daily routine work and should not go unnoticed. Here, managers have the opportunity to show recognition more often.

Verbal personal praise or in front of employees is the "smallest unit" of recognition. A written note or an e-mail of appreciation is always well received. They don't take much time, but their impact should not be underestimated. This type of recognition - also known as a "kudo" - should always be prompt, authentic and clearly state the reason for the praise. The comment "good performance", for example, is a general statement, whereas the alternative "great presentation on topic xy" clearly states the context. (kuveno 2023) A leadership-sensitive company makes sure to give such positive feedback to diverse employees time and again.

It is always possible to give special consideration to leadership by recognizing its promotion. Bonuses are one possibility. Has someone been able to make contact with a new customer or supplier group with a focus on leadership? A separate remuneration amount is conceivable for this.

Employees who have rendered outstanding services to the topic of leadership can also be named "Employee of the Month". Consideration can be given to combining this with a bonus.

Appreciation can also be shown in the form of invitations to a meal or a course. Perhaps a department has made a special contribution to leadership - then that would be an option.

Managers can promote recognition as part of the corporate culture by repeatedly encouraging employees to recognize each other's achievements. In this way, praise is not only hierarchy-dependent, but also takes place within the company peer groups.

Giving recognition to diverse people counteracts an often deeply rooted prejudice that they often experience in society, namely that they have a problematic attribute and have to overcome it themselves. However, they do not achieve the performance that diverse talents achieve, even though they are diverse. They achieve it because they are who they are, with all their attributes. The inclusion that needs to be achieved is in the hands and responsibility of society, of which companies are a large part.

Literature

Synergy-through-diversity 2023, D&I for reading, retrieved 28.05.2024, https://synergie-durch-vielfalt.de/diversity-themen/religion

HAZ 2023, Hannoversche Allgemeine Zeitung from November 23, 2023

Diversity Charter 2023, Future factor diversity, accessed on 28.05.2024, https://www.charta-der-vielfalt.de/fileadmin/user_upload/Studien_Publikationen_Charta/Charta_der_Vielfa lt_-_KMU-Brosch%C3%BCre_2020.pdf

Kofa 2023, DiversityManagement.pdf, accessed 28.05.2024, https://www.kofa.de/personalarbeit/unternehmenskultur/diversity-management/

Diversity Charter 2023, Future factor diversity, accessed on 28.05.2024, https://www.charta-der-vielfalt.de/fileadmin/user_upload/Studien_Publikationen_Charta/Charta_der_Vielfa lt_-_KMU-Brosch%C3%BCre_2020.pdf

Agency-young-heart 2021, MEASURES FOR DIVERSITY, retrieved 28.05.2024, https://www.agentur-jungesherz.de/blog/massnahmen-fuer-diversity-wie-unternehmen-diversity-foerdern-koennen/

akademie 2022, LUNCH & LEARN DOCUMENTATION, accessed 28.05.2024, https://akademie.hshl.de/wp-content/uploads/2022/ 09/Lunch-Learn.pdf

Business Dictionary 2023, Definition: What is "mediation"? Retrieved 28.05.2024, 2023https://wirtschaftslexikon.gabler.de/definition/mediation-39811

bmev.de 2023, Elder Mediation, accessed 28.05.2024, https://www.bmev.de/mediation/einsatzbereiche/elder-mediation.html, Elder Mediation

gotscharek-company 2023, Self-directed-coaching-through-collegial-consulting, accessed 28.05.2024, https://www.gotscharek-company.com/blog-1/120-selbstgesteuertes-coaching-durch-kollegiale-beratung

Diversity Charter 2023, From vision to everyday life, accessed 28.05.2024, https://www.charta-der-

vielfalt.de/fileadmin/user_upload/Studien_Publikationen_Charta/Charta_der_Vielfa
lt_-_KMU-Brosch%C3%BCre_2020.pdf

CSR 2023, Act on Corporate Due Diligence in Supply Chains, retrieved
28.05.2024, https://www.csr-in-deutschland.de/DE/Wirtschaft-
Menschenrechte/Gesetz-ueber-die-unternehmerischen-Sorgfaltspflichten-in-
Lieferketten/gesetz-ueber-die-unternehmerischen-sorgfaltspflichten-in-lieferketten.html

atlassian 2023, Team management and leadership, accessed 28.05.2024,
https://www.atlassian.com/de/work-management/team-management-and-
leadership/team-management-strategies/employee-recognition

kuveno 2023, Translation Kudos to German: Knowledge and meaning of terms,
retrieved 28.05.2024, https://kunveno.de/blog/%C3%BCbersetzung-kudos-auf-
deutsch

8 Summary and conclusion

In today's hyperconnected global marketplace, the integration of diverse perspectives through hyper leadership is not merely a moral imperative but an economic necessity. Organizations that embrace hyper agility while fostering inclusive environments create sustainable competitive advantages that extend far beyond traditional metrics. This transformation requires dismantling outdated patriarchal and rigid hierarchical structures in favor of dynamic, responsive organizational models that can adapt rapidly to changing market conditions.

The convergence of hyper leadership and hyper agility creates a powerful synergy where diversity becomes a catalyst for innovation and organizational resilience. When companies leverage diverse talent pools through adaptive leadership frameworks, they unlock enhanced research capabilities, creative problem-solving approaches, and market intelligence that directly translate to improved financial performance. This inclusive approach to organizational agility doesn't compromise efficiency—it amplifies it by harnessing the collective intelligence of varied perspectives and experiences.

The evidence is clear: organizations that successfully implement hyper leadership principles while maintaining hyper agility not only strengthen democratic workplace processes and create more humane working environments but also achieve superior business outcomes. The future belongs to organizations that can seamlessly integrate diversity, agility, and inclusive leadership into their core operational DNA, transforming what was once viewed as a compliance requirement into a fundamental driver of innovation, growth, and long-term success.

8.1 Importance of the development of diverse teams

The inclusion of leadership is not just a process that strengthens democratic decisions and treats individuals equally. leadership is an economic necessity that enables companies to assert themselves on national and international markets. Leadership also brings competitive advantages. Promising operational structures require working in teams. Collaboration in diverse teams brings the following advantages:

1. The company saves costs

Good inclusion increases employee motivation because there is a respectful working atmosphere. In addition, costs resulting from complaints against discrimination and unlawful disadvantage are avoided.

2. Greater flexibility

Leadership in teams leads to more flexible reactions than in rather cumbersome homogeneous groups. Flexibility is becoming increasingly important in a time of diverse structural changes.

3. Better problem solving

In diverse teams, creativity increases and with it the likelihood of solving problems effectively. The power of innovation is greater.

4. Easier recruitment

Diverse teams offer far greater potential that HR management can draw on. They can be formed at short notice and quickly reconstituted with other members.

5. Customer obsession

A diverse workforce can better serve a diverse customer base. Improved customer orientation opens up new markets. Intercultural knowledge and skills are becoming increasingly important in international business relationships. Diverse people avoid misunderstandings on both a factual and interpersonal level. They are therefore indispensable as team members.

7. Corporate image

The company's image is improving because customers are increasingly taking ethical and social criteria into account when making purchasing decisions.

A company is therefore well served if it has many diverse members in its talent pool.

8.2 Most important findings

Changing framework conditions in economic and political contexts play a major role in the growing importance of Hyper Leadership. These include:

- globalization
- sales markets and jobs that are becoming more international
- demographic change
- a changed understanding of gender roles
- increased self-confidence among people with disabilities
- increased self-confidence among people who belong to the LGBTQ+ group
- growing ethnic diversity through migration
- changed values and greater importance of the individual
- legal requirements
- a clientele characterized by increasing diversity
- cooperation between companies across national borders

Leadership and inclusion are factors that can no longer be neglected in innovative companies if serious disadvantages are to be avoided in a globalized market. This requires a corporate organization that takes the well-being of employees into account alongside a differentiated customer focus. The corresponding culture includes a natural appreciation of diverse people.

In a well-functioning leadership management system, personnel development is geared towards leadership. Appropriate tools and procedures are used to find and retain diverse talent within the company. At the same time, internal conscious or unconscious prejudices are successfully reduced. The working atmosphere is characterized by mutual appreciation and a democratic attitude. Various measures are used to support employees in developing their professional, social and personal skills.

In order to promote mutual understanding, organizational structures such as the formation of cross-teams are practiced. The workplaces are set up in such a way that non-diverse and diverse people can feel comfortable. Hierarchical levels are kept as flat as possible to support creativity, inclusion, collaboration and team building. Leadership is continuously promoted and the implementation of leadership in the company is evaluated and further developed. Public relations work consistently and continuously includes diverse people in all presentations. Stakeholders are at least informed about the implementation of leadership and, in the best case, they themselves support leadership in working life.

Leadership in the workforce is the be-all and end-all of leadership management. The company has a culture of interaction based on mutual respect. Constructive and open communication is cultivated at all levels. Managers make their decisions transparent. They act as role models.

Leadership management is based on bringing together different attitudes, experiences, knowledge and skills and utilizing the resulting synergy effect. The aim is to ensure fairness throughout the entire workforce. All employees should therefore be satisfied with their work and feel like a valuable member of a corporate community with common goals. No person should have to remain in the same job once they have moved on. Professional options are available for resolving conflict situations. Management is not afraid to involve external help. This applies, for example, to further training and other measures that the company cannot provide on its own.

Leadership includes several dimensions. Although women make up around half of the population, in many cases they need to be included in leadership management because they are underrepresented. The gender ratio is particularly unbalanced among managers. In many countries, the picture is the same with regard to people with non-white skin color, e.g. still strongly in the USA. In terms of age, it is still the case that older people have fewer opportunities on the labor market. Leadership also includes sexual orientation and religion. Furthermore, people with disabilities still experience exclusion. In addition to these classic characteristics that lead to the perception and often negative assessment of leadership, there are also secondary dispositions. For example, social background and educational background also play a role, so that such components must also be taken into account. Leadership management is therefore always a contribution to making society fairer and more humane.

Leadership management also leads to appropriate treatment of the entire workforce. Communication channels for employees ensure good social interaction. A variety of offers - such as sports facilities and different menus in the canteen - cater to the needs of employees.

Leadership in companies leads to positive operational results. Diverse teams make more informed and competent decisions than homogeneous working groups because many different aspects flow into a project. This has a serious impact on the development and further development of products and services. Companies can therefore intervene more effectively in the market, achieve better balance sheets and prove to be more resilient.

Leadership and sustainability go hand in hand. Sustainable companies are increasingly in demand because customers are attaching more and more importance to ecologically and economically responsible products. In the knowledge society, it quickly becomes apparent if an item has been produced under precarious working conditions. The goal of producing sustainable products requires interdisciplinary cooperation and the involvement of diverse people.

Companies need a corporate ethic in which leadership, inclusion, a sense of justice and sustainability are given priority. This attitude is verbalized in the corporate mission statement. A value chain that includes inclusion has a positive impact on the conservation of resources and ultimately on the company's success. Within the company, social participation and a high level of involvement contribute to this. Representation for diverse people should be guaranteed, as should a gender-neutral attitude. Outside the company, an innovative company should participate in social activities.

So far, risk-taking companies have been more open to inclusion. However, SMEs will not be able to survive due to the shortage of skilled workers alone if they ignore the requirements of an evolving social and economic transformation. Even if they have fewer options than large companies, they can still realize many of the opportunities presented here. After all, technological and demographic change will not pass them by.

When HR development establishes leadership management, it creates an overall concept. The aim is to create a non-discriminatory, respectful working environment in which personal leadership is reflected at all levels of the company. Such a concept is based on recognizing, respecting and utilizing the differences and similarities of the people in the workforce. Its principles are visible and tangible throughout the entire structure of the company and are reflected in the guidelines. An inclusion-oriented concept fulfills at least the following criteria:

- development opportunities for pluralism
- appreciation, support and inclusion of leadership as a fundamental basis for work
- high degree of integrative cooperation, e.g. in networks
- no occurrence or the consistent combating of internal discrimination, whether direct or indirect
- constructive communication in teams as well as across hierarchies

Basic approaches to Leadership management are:

1. The approach at management level

The management level must want leadership management and ensure that it is implemented. It cannot be assumed that all companies will be able to implement everything presented here overnight and in a short space of time. In many medium-sized companies in particular, central objectives and values will probably continue to be defined only at management level. Leadership management should therefore be seen as a matter for managers. They should consider the benefits of employing diverse people and actively and transparently communicate their recruitment and promotion.

2. The approach in the workforce

Leadership management can only be practiced successfully if all employees are involved and convinced. This requires well-functioning communication channels. Working groups and networks are important inclusion tools.

3. The holistic approach

Hyper Leadership: Catalyzing Organizational Agility Through Diversity

In today's rapidly evolving business landscape, the intersection of Hyper Leadership and organizational agility has become increasingly crucial for sustainable success. This chapter explores how Hyper Leadership—a leadership approach that embraces and leverages diversity in all its forms—acts as a catalyst for creating unprecedented levels of workforce agility.

The Foundation of Hyper Leadership

Hyper Leadership emerges from the convergence of multiple transformative forces in our modern business environment. Globalization, demographic shifts, evolving gender roles, increased self-advocacy among marginalized groups, and cross-border collaboration have fundamentally altered how organizations must operate to remain competitive. This leadership paradigm recognizes that diversity isn't merely about meeting quotas or fulfilling legal requirements—it's about harnessing the collective potential of a varied workforce to create adaptive, responsive organizations.

The Agility Advantage

When Hyper Leadership principles are effectively implemented, they naturally foster organizational agility through several key mechanisms:

1. Enhanced Decision-Making Through Diverse Perspectives

Organizations practicing Hyper Leadership benefit from the convergence of varied viewpoints and experiences. When teams include members from different cultural backgrounds, gender identities, age groups, and ability levels, they develop more comprehensive problem-solving approaches. This diversity of thought enables faster adaptation to market changes and more innovative solutions to complex challenges.

2. Flattened Hierarchies and Fluid Communication

Hyper Leadership promotes flatter organizational structures that facilitate rapid information flow and decision-making. By reducing hierarchical barriers, organizations can respond more quickly to changing circumstances. Cross-functional teams can form and dissolve as needed, creating a natural state of organizational fluidity that supports agility.

3. Cultural Intelligence and Market Responsiveness

In an increasingly globalized marketplace, organizations with diverse workforces possess inherent advantages in understanding and responding to varied customer needs. Hyper Leadership cultivates this cultural intelligence, enabling companies to pivot quickly in response to market shifts and customer preferences across different demographics and regions.

Building Blocks of Hyper Agility

The transformation from traditional organizational structures to hyper-agile entities requires several key components:

Inclusive Decision-Making Frameworks

Hyper leaders establish systems that actively incorporate diverse perspectives into decision-making processes. This might include:
- Cross-functional steering committees
- Rotating leadership roles
- Multi-level feedback mechanisms
- Inclusive project teams

Adaptive Skill Development

Organizations under Hyper Leadership prioritize continuous learning and skill development across all employee groups. This focus on perpetual growth creates a workforce that can readily adapt to new challenges and opportunities.

Flexible Work Structures

The implementation of adaptable work arrangements accommodates diverse needs while promoting organizational agility:

- Remote work options
- Flexible scheduling
- Job sharing opportunities
- Cross-training initiatives

The Synergy Effect

Perhaps the most powerful aspect of Hyper Leadership is its ability to create synergistic effects between diversity and agility. When leaders actively promote inclusion and appreciation of differences, they create an environment where:

1. Innovation flourishes through the cross-pollination of ideas
2. Resilience increases due to varied problem-solving approaches
3. Market responsiveness improves through deeper understanding of diverse customer bases
4. Adaptability becomes ingrained in organizational culture

Measuring Impact and Success

Organizations implementing Hyper Leadership principles should monitor several key indicators to assess their progress toward greater agility:

Quantitative Metrics
- Speed of decision-making
- Time to market for new initiatives
- Employee engagement scores across diverse groups

- Innovation metrics (new products, services, or processes)

Qualitative Indicators
- Quality of cross-functional collaboration
- Effectiveness of knowledge sharing
- Cultural adaptation capabilities
- Employee satisfaction with inclusion efforts

Challenges and Solutions

While the benefits of Hyper Leadership are clear, organizations often face challenges in implementation. Common obstacles include:

Resistance to Change: Implement gradual changes while clearly communicating benefits and providing support structures for adaptation.

Communication Barriers: Develop multilingual and multicultural communication strategies that accommodate different styles and preferences.

Integration Difficulties: Create mentorship programs and cross-cultural training initiatives to facilitate better understanding and collaboration.

Future Implications

As markets continue to evolve and workforce demographics shift further, the importance of Hyper Leadership in fostering organizational agility will only increase. Organizations that successfully implement these principles will find themselves better positioned to:
- Navigate market uncertainties
- Attract and retain diverse talent
- Respond to changing customer needs
- Drive innovation through inclusive practices

Hyper Agility: The Starting Point for Organizational Transformation

Hyper agility emerges as the foundational solution that enables organizations to harness the full potential of diverse leadership while navigating complex market demands. This comprehensive approach to organizational flexibility provides the structural framework necessary to transform diversity from a static concept into a dynamic competitive advantage. The journey toward hyper agility begins with three critical starting points: first, conducting a comprehensive organizational assessment to identify current rigidities and barriers that prevent diverse perspectives from contributing effectively; second, implementing pilot programs that create cross-functional, diverse teams with decision-making authority to test new approaches on smaller scales; and third, establishing rapid feedback loops that allow for continuous adjustment and learning. Organizations should begin by selecting one high-impact area—such as product development or customer service—where diverse perspectives can immediately demonstrate value, then gradually expand these principles across all operational levels. The key is to start with manageable changes that build momentum and demonstrate clear results, while simultaneously developing the cultural infrastructure that supports both inclusive leadership and organizational responsiveness. This initial phase requires commitment from leadership to model hyper agile behaviors, invest in necessary technological platforms that facilitate collaboration across diverse teams, and create psychological safety where experimentation and rapid iteration are not only accepted but encouraged. Success in implementing hyper agility depends on understanding that this is not a destination but a continuous evolution toward more adaptive, inclusive, and ultimately more successful organizational structures.

Conclusion

Hyper Leadership represents more than just a management philosophy—it's a crucial approach for building agile, resilient organizations capable of thriving in an increasingly complex business environment. By embracing diversity and fostering inclusive practices, organizations can develop the agility needed to navigate future challenges while maintaining competitive advantages in global markets.

Hyper Leadership is a company-wide issue and a structural factor. If you introduce this principle, it must be reflected in all processes. Leadership must become a natural and indispensable part of the entire company, from corporate culture to operations. Supporting measures such as training and mentoring help here. External support such as coaching is also useful.

Hyper Leadership management is easiest to establish in companies (as well as in organizations) that

- generate growth,
- conduct research,
- take ethical principles seriously,
- show flexibility and
- make decentralized decisions.

Hyper Leadership can only be incorporated in stages, but there must be an overall concept and the courage to adopt new methods and new forms of organization, including new business models with new ways of thinking. Hyper Leadership management requires long-term introduction and establishment. It includes the path from the mere avoidance of disadvantages and discrimination to an appreciative culture that includes leadership as a matter of course.

In its entirety, this book represents a vision of the future. But a promising future should begin in the present.